AVE 0250

Zen
MASTER CLASS

Zen
MASTER CLASS

A COURSE IN ZEN WISDOM

from

TRADITIONAL MASTERS

Quest Books
Theosophical Publishing House
Wheaton, Illinois ◆ Chennai (Madras), India

When everything is seen as One,
we return to the source
and stay where we have always been.

Copyright © 2002 Godsfield Press
Text copyright © 2002 Stephen Hodge

First Quest Edition 2002
Copublished with Godsfield Press 2002

The Theosophical Publishing House
P.O. Box 270
Wheaton, Illinois 60189-0270

Designed for Godsfield Press by The Bridgewater Book Company

Library of Congress Cataloging-in-Publication Data

Hodge, Stephen.

Zen Master class: A Course in Zen wisdom from Traditional Masters: For Meditators at Every Level / Stephen Hodge.

p.   cm.

Includes bibliographical references and index.

ISBN 0-8356-0818-2

1. Zen Buddhism--Doctrines.   2. Priests, Zen--Biography.   I. Title.

BQ9268.3 .H63   2002

294.3'927--dc21

2002017704

Printed and bound in China

QUEST BOOKS are published by The Theosophical Society in America, Wheaton, Illinois 60189-0270, a branch of a world fellowship, a membership organization dedicated to the promotion of the unity of humanity and the encouragement of the study of religion, philosophy, and science, to the end that we may better understand ourselves and our place in the universe. The Society stands for complete freedom of individual search and belief.

For further information about its activities,write, call 1-800-669-1571, e-mail olcott@theosmail.net,or consult its Web page: http://www.theosophical.org

The Theosophical Publishing House is aided by the generous support of THE KERN FOUNDATION, a trust established by Herbert A. Kern and dedicated to Theosophical education.

Contents

"There is no Buddha and no Dharma: If they exist at all, they are just empty

words!" This provocative statement was made by Linji, one of the most revered Zen Masters of China. Some Zen Masters went even further, telling their disciples that statues of the Buddha should be chopped up and burned along with scrolls of the Buddhist scriptures. Yet this apparent iconoclasm is not what is seems. Quite simply, Zen Buddhism would not exist without the Buddha, his Enlightenment, and the teachings that arose from his experience, called the *Dharma*. As we'll discover as we explore the lives, teachings, and lessons of the illustrious Chinese and Japanese Zen Masters in this book, the provocative statements, eccentric behavior, and non-traditional methods characteristic of Zen were aimed at awakening the Buddha-nature inherent within each person, a goal all practitioners of Buddhism share. So, we might ask to start with, who was the Buddha and what is the nature of his message?

Siddhartha Gautama, who was destined to become the Buddha, was born as a prince during the fifth century BCE at Lumbini in present-day Nepal. Because it had been predicted that Gautama would become either a great emperor or a great sage when he reached adulthood, his father determined to do whatever he could to assure that his son would have a political rather than a spiritual destiny. To protect his son from religious influences, Gautama's father made sure that he spent his youth and early adulthood within the luxurious confines of the palace grounds. When he was grown, Gautama married and had a son of his own.

Despite the pleasures of his life, Gautama began to wonder about the lives of ordinary people outside the palace walls. He ordered his charioteer to take him out secretly so he could see the world for himself. What Gautama beheld on his four excursions had a profound impact on him. On the first trip, he saw an old person; on the next, a sick and diseased man; on the third, a corpse being carried to be cremated. In confusion, he asked his charioteer about these sights and was told simply that each was part of the harsh reality of human existence. "Will these things happen to me?" he asked. "Inevitably," he was told. In despair and horror, Gautama made a final trip. On this occasion, he saw a wandering holy man sitting serenely in the midst of the crowds.

Inspired by the sight of that wandering sage, Gautama made up his mind to leave the palace to seek an answer to the decay and death that awaited him and all beings. Late one night, he abandoned his finery, shaved

禪

off his hair, and left the palace to become one of the many spiritual seekers who flourished in India at that time. On his wanderings, Gautama visited many of the noted teachers of his day, staying with them to learn what he could. However, no one had the answers he was seeking. Later, he wandered by himself or in the company of a few companions, at times torturing his body with severe ascetic practices. Yet still he was unable to reach the serenity that he sought.

Finally, six years after he had left his father's palace, Gautama found himself on the banks of the River Nairanjana, a small tributary of the Ganges. Sitting at the base of a tree, Gautama entered a profound state of meditation. As dawn broke the next morning, he achieved the breakthrough he had been seeking—profound and blissful Enlightenment. From that day on, he was known by the title, Buddha, the Enlightened One.

禪

He spent the remainder of his life teaching others about the insights he had acquired and explaining how they might free themselves from frustration and misery by achieving Enlightenment as well.

Over the next fifty years, the Buddha gave many different teachings, each suited to the ability and interests of his audience. Though the content and style of these teachings varied, they contained a number of core ideas that comprise the basic beliefs of Buddhists down to the present day. It is important to note that everything that the Buddha taught was based on what he had personally experienced rather than some revelation from God. He also insisted that rather than blindly accepting his words out of reverence, people should find out the truth of his teachings for themselves. Try what I teach and see if it works for you, he told his followers.

Three Principles and Three Strategies

At a basic level, the Buddha taught three interconnected principles concerning human life: suffering, impermanence, and the absence of an ego-self. The idea that human existence is pervaded by misery and frustration can be difficult for Western people to accept. Yet a single television newscast provides ample evidence that humankind is awash in misery worldwide and that we are a lucky and privileged few. But even those of us who think ourselves immune from extreme suffering are often confronted, sometimes unexpectedly, with the pain that characterizes human existence. Careful reflection reveals that despite material comforts, we all experience emotional unhappiness, boredom, loneliness, and insecurity.

Why, the Buddha wondered next, is human suffering so pervasive and universal? The answer, he realized, is quite simple: Suffering exists because all things are impermanent. Although we know intellectually that everything is always changing, most of us conduct our lives as though everything that is will last forever. According to the Buddha, the misery and frustration we experience arises because of the mistaken expectation of permanence. While we are happy, we think that we will always be so; when we lose what we have grown attached to, we experience the pain of loss. The truth is, that no matter how bad or how good things are, everything is changing, from the great mountains to our everyday thoughts and emotions. Accepting this truth reduces our suffering tremendously.

禪

The third characteristic of human existence the Buddha taught is that there is no such thing as an unchanging, independent ego-self. Through meditation techniques designed specifically for the purpose, we can come to see that there is no part of the body or mind that can be identified as the ego-self. When we are faced with the sense that things are not as we would have them be, the ego-self seems to emerge to defend us against the lack of control we have over our lives. When we try to hold on to things that are dear to us or experience pain when we lose them, we entrench ourselves further behind the protection of the ego-self in a vain attempt to ward off discomfort. Clinging to this false sense of identity leads only to greater attachment and to more suffering and frustration.

Looking at this process, the Buddha concluded that people fail to understand the dynamics at work in their lives and consequently adopt strategies that can result only in failure. Indeed, he said, ignorance entraps people in a vicious circle of desperate measures and unwanted results. In its attempt to protect itself from new

禅

and potentially upsetting experiences, the ego-mind employs one of three strategies: When we are faced with something that seems threatening or uncomfortable, we react with aversion and try to shut it out or destroy it. Alternately, if we believe that something can increase our pleasure or power, we attempt to control it through attachment and subordinate it to our wishes and desires. If we fail in these two strategies, we ignore whatever is happening in the hope that it will disappear of its own accord. From these three strategies arises a host of negative and destructive emotions, such as jealousy, lust, greed, and spite.

These negative emotions and their positive opposites, such as kindness, patience, and generosity, motivate nearly all human actions. Because our actions are charged with emotional energy, the Buddha taught that the effects of our actions go beyond the immediate results of which we are aware. In fact, every thought, word, and deed imprints some of its energy on our mindstream. Positive actions leave positive imprints; negative actions leave negative imprints. The energy of these imprints will be released at some time in the future when circumstances trigger experiences that reflect the energy pattern of the original motivation. Though the specifics may vary, negative motivations and actions always lead to distressing and painful experiences, while positive ones have the opposite effect. Because appropriate circumstances often fail to arise during our present lifetime, the Buddha taught that we are subject to rebirth, lifetime after lifetime, until the energy of all the imprints on our mindstream has been exhausted. Unless we take action to short-circuit this process, each lifetime gives us the opportunity to create more and more negative imprints so that the cycle is virtually unending. Such are the workings of cause and effect, which the Buddha termed *karma*.

Meditation for Tranquility and Insight

Living a moral life can help us lessen our burden of negative karmic energy and ease some of the discomfort we experience as human beings. However, the Buddha also taught that to bring the whole process of karma and rebirth to an end, meditation is essential. As Buddhism developed over the centuries, many techniques for meditation were devised, all of which arise from two basic types, both central to the practice of Zen. The aim of the first type is calmness and tranquility. The Buddha knew that our everyday minds are filled with a torrent of thoughts and emotions, most of very short duration. These act as a kind of smoke screen that prevents us from focusing our minds on anything that might undermine our carefully crafted illusion that all is well. When we learn to concentrate our minds on a single positive and wholesome object, such as an image of the Buddha, a sacred sound, or the flow of our breathing, we gradually learn to quiet our thoughts, control outbursts of negative emotion, and experience a degree of peace and tranquility.

Once we have gained the ability to focus our attention, we can practice the second type of meditation, which aims at the development of insight. The Buddha taught that the root of our predicament lies in the fact that we do not perceive anything in the world as it truly is. Instead, we live in a delusional pseudoreality created by us through the ego-mind. Meditation can train us to see things as they actually are. The many meditation techniques with this aim are intended to help us cut through the confusion with the scalpel of insight, which we grasp by firmly grounding ourselves in the Buddha's teachings on the three characteristics of existence.

The process of meditation to develop insight does not consist of thinking about suffering or impermanence directly but rather in techniques that help us to recognize that we have chosen to ignore these all-pervasive aspects of existence. Eventually, we come to see that our usual strategies based on the demands of the ego-mind are unreliable and lead only to disappointment. Instead of acting as though everything is permanent, we abandon ourselves to the stream of change. Instead of seeking to avoid suffering, we understand its causes and the ways we bring it upon ourselves. Instead of holding tightly to the belief in a self-existent ego-mind, we see that everything is interdependent, each event arising because of a host of mutually interacting causes and conditions.

禅

The Monastic Tradition

These key doctrines of Buddhism were transmitted down the ages by followers who committed themselves formally to the study and practice of the Buddha's methods. In the first few centuries after the Buddha's passing, his followers applied themselves zealously to the search for peace and liberation from the cycle of rebirths propelled by karma. But as time went by and the Buddhist community grew in size, various groups of monks emerged, each with their own agenda. Some continued to devote their energies to meditation as had generations of monks before them, quietly seeking their own liberation. Others pursued scholastic study of the *sutras*, scriptures that recorded the teachings of the Buddha. They extracted the doctrines scattered throughout the texts and arranged them into convenient lists. To these they then added comments and explanatory material. Rather than practicing meditation, these monks focused on subtle doctrinal distinctions and on debates with other scholars.

A third group of monks acknowledged that meditation and study were important, but argued that such pursuits were limited as they tended to become ends in themselves. They took the life and career of the Buddha himself as model for a new spiritual ideal: the bodhisattva. A *bodhisattva* is a person who aims to achieve supreme Enlightenment in order to help other beings by relieving their suffering. This new movement appealed to both clerical and lay people and to both men and women. Its adherents termed their approach the *Mahayana*, the Great Way, in contrast to the less ambitious aims of monks who worked to achieve their own liberation. They termed this more limited approach the *Hinayana*, the Lesser Way. Mahayana Buddhism, which emerged as a distinct movement around the early first century BCE, taught that the chief concern of a bodhisattva should be the simultaneous cultivation of compassion and insight. This form of Buddhism flourished in India until the Muslim onslaught in the eleventh century CE. By that time, its teachings had spread to many other Asian countries, such as Tibet, China, Korea, and Japan, where they continued in various forms down the centuries to the present day.

Mahayana scholars found evidence in the Buddha's teachings that all beings are endowed with the capacity to achieve Enlightenment. Some Mahayana adherents, including practitioners of Zen, believe that Enlightenment,

禅

the awakening of the Buddha-mind or Buddha-nature, is our natural state, but has been covered over by layers of negative emotions and distorted thoughts. According to this view, Enlightenment is not something that we must acquire a bit at a time, but a state that can occur instantly when we cut through the dense veil of mental and emotional obscurations.

This book presents key aspects of the lives and teachings of twenty great Zen Masters, some well-known and some less so, who show us by example how we might free ourselves from misery and gain the peace and wisdom of Enlightenment. Imagine as you read that you are sitting at the feet of these masters, hearing their words and trying for yourself the techniques and methods they taught. As with any new skill, don't be discouraged if you do not get instant results. Buddhist practice does change things, even if you don't notice at first. Some readers may wish to supplement this book with the support and encouragement found at a Buddhist center, but you can make good progress working on your own, provided you are diligent and honest with yourself.

May the lessons in this Zen Master Class help you find peace and happiness!

禪

Bodhidharma *(470-534)*

A special transmission outside the scriptures;
No dependence upon words and letters;
Direct pointing at the mind;
Seeing into one's nature and the attainment of buddhahood.

In the early years of the sixth century CE, a solitary Indian monk, who was to set in motion extraordinary changes in the Buddhist world, landed on the southern shores of China. This traveling monk was Bodhidharma, later recognized as the twenty-eighth Indian patriarch of Zen and the first in China.

What kind of spiritual world did Bodhidharma find in China? During the five hundred years that preceded his arrival, Buddhism had made an enormous impact on Chinese life. By the sixth century, a thousand years after Shakyamuni Buddha, China had hundreds of Buddhist temples, a monastic population of many thousands, and fervent lay devotees ranging from the emperor down to humble peasants.

Though its profound meditative practices and complex metaphysics were beyond all but a few rare practitioners, Mahayana Buddhism offered more humble ways of gradual spiritual advancement. Aware of the strenuous effort needed to make progress toward Enlightenment, many people followed a more practical path. They believed that generosity toward monks and nuns, endowing new temples and monasteries, copying scriptures, and leading a moral life would generate sufficient merit, as they termed positive karma, for them to achieve a happy and favorable rebirth. Others were attracted to the popular Pure Land school of Buddhism, in which recollecting the image and name of a Buddha ensured rebirth in a special paradise where conditions were right for the final journey to Enlightenment. All in

all, Buddhism had become quite settled and comfortable in China. But this reassuring style of Buddhist practice was rudely awakened by the Zen school founded by Bodhidharma.

So, who was this Bodhidharma? The answer is simple: We don't really know. Like many founders of innovative spiritual movements, much of his life is shrouded in mystery, like the misty scenes in a Chinese ink painting. Pruning away the pious legends surrounding his life, the bare historical facts can be summarized in a few lines. Bodhidharma was probably born in southern India, although some early sources mention Persia instead. Following Indian custom, he would have become a monk in his youth, practicing the Mahayana Buddhist teachings.

After reaching China as a middle-aged man in 520, Bodhidharma traveled around the country, eventually making his way north and settling at the Shaolin Monastery on Mount Song in the kingdom of Wei around 527. Here he passed nine years in intense silent meditation, waiting, it is said, until students of the right caliber turned up. Eventually, a handful of such people—including the future second patriarch, Huike—arrived and became Bodhidharma's disciples. Huike must have been his most outstanding student, and it was to him that Bodhidharma passed the spiritual lineage of Zen with the visible insignia of that status, the bowl and robe. It is probable that Bodhidharma remained at Shaolin Monastery until his death some years later.

An episode that occurred soon after Bodhidharma's arrival in China helps explain why this seemingly uneventful life made such an impact on Chinese Buddhism. While visiting the southern Chinese kingdom of Liang, Bodhidharma was granted an audience with the emperor Wu. As we have seen, the Chinese laid great emphasis on acts of generosity and patronage as central to their practice of Buddhism. The emperor told Bodhidharma that he had built many temples, sponsored the translation of texts, and supported the ordination of monks—all acts that conventional Buddhism taught guaranteed him much merit.

"So," the emperor asked, "just how much merit have I accumulated?"

"None whatsoever," Bodhidharma replied.

Bodhidharma went on to explain that good deeds produce only transitory rewards, such as rebirth in a paradise, because merit itself is transitory and devoid of ultimate reality. Naturally, the emperor Wu asked Bodhidharma to explain what brings genuine merit.

禅

"Genuine merit comes about only in the purity and aware-ness of perfect Enlightenment, which is possible only after your body and mind have become tranquil because you have realized that they, too, are devoid of ultimate reality."

Poor Emperor Wu! Obviously he had not been keeping up with his study of the Mahayana *sutras*, the recorded dialogues or sermons of the Buddha. In fact, Bodhidharma's explanation is a commonplace teaching of many Mahayana scriptures. Meritorious deeds are fine, but if they are done with the expec-tation of gaining merit, they do not assure liberation from the painful cycle of birth and death. Emperor Wu's understanding of the Dharma, was limited by his expectations; like an investor in the stock market, he wanted to know how much his merit port-folio was worth, thus revealing himself to be a spiritual materialist.

Baffled, Wu tried another tack with Bodhidharma.

"What, then, is the primary principle of holiness?" he asked, perhaps trying out some Buddhist jargon to impress Bodhidharma. If he was hoping for a simple answer, he was in for a surprise.

"There is only emptiness, no holiness!" Bodhidharma retorted.

We can imagine a confused Emperor Wu shaking his head, perhaps wondering if his interpreter had missed something. He made one last attempt to get this impertinent stranger to talk some sense.

"Who is now before me?" he asked.

"Don't know!" Bodhidharma replied, ending the discussion.

The circumstances may have been somewhat different, but like Pontius Pilate four hundred years earlier in another land facing another religious eccentric, Emperor Wu washed his hands of Bodhidharma. He lacked the spiritual development to under-stand that Bodhidharma was offering him a higher understanding than the predictable and easy path of merit collecting to which he was accustomed, an understanding that would have moved him further and quicker along the path to Enlightenment.

If this exchange is typical of Bodhidharma's method, we can imagine the impact the inspiring directness of his teachings must have had upon people who sought the quickest way to achieving the Buddhism's ultimate goal—Enlightenment.

禪

TEACHINGS *Entry Through Practice*

So what were Bodhidharma's most important teachings? According to a short work attributed to him, the Two Ways of Entrance, the path to Enlightenment has two approaches: entry through practice and entry through meditation.

Entry through practice is a simple program of emotional and intellectual development to be cultivated in daily life, especially during those times when we are not engaged in formal meditation. Four aspects are involved: patient acceptance, equanimity, determination, and insight—positive qualities that are extolled in many Mahayana Buddhist scriptures.

Patient acceptance means that we are able to endure any ills that befall us and accept without rancor the rigors of the path and its implications for our lives. Patience is particularly useful in overcoming anger. According to the Buddha, anger is the most destructive of all negative emotions. One moment of anger is like a spark that will consume a vast heap of goodness accumulated over countless lifetimes. Difficult though it may be, we should train ourselves to endure patiently whatever others do to us, without resentment. It helps to remember that we created the cause for whatever happens to us through the dynamics of our karmic actions in the past. Patient acceptance also implies that we avoid giving ourselves over to feelings of fatigue and despair because of difficulties we encounter on the path. In other words, we should be patient with ourselves as well as with others.

禅

Equanimity is a balanced attitude that avoids the extremes of attraction and aversion. It enables us to overcome bias and prejudice in our responses to others and functions as an antidote to pride and partiality. As the Buddha taught, pride often occupies center stage in the workings of the ego-self because of our inherent belief that we are more important or more valuable than others. Because of pride, we are likely to feel hostile toward those who seem to threaten our sense of importance. We also may be overattached to pleasant situations and to people who seem to promise protection for the ego-self from change, and we may react with jealousy toward others when we feel that we have somehow missed out on what is rightfully "ours." Thus a lack of equanimity leads us to favor people who seem to advance our ego-self and boost our self-importance, and to act with aversion toward those who endanger it despite the fact that such feelings may be entirely groundless.

The Buddhist view is that all beings are equal. Several arguments are given to prove this contention. Most basically, all beings are endowed with Buddha-nature or the intrinsic potential for Enlightenment and are hence worthy of respect. It is sometimes difficult to come to terms with this idea when we consider very evil people. Perhaps the best course is to think of such people as suffering from a grave sickness. This view accords well with the Buddha's own approach to the human condition. The Buddha taught that any attitude and its resulting actions that brings harm to others is a form of disease akin to insanity. When we read in the newspaper that somebody has been murdered by a person suffering from psychotic delusions, we may feel sadness and anger that the perpetrator has been allowed to live unsupervised and untreated by society, but normally we accept that the person is not responsible for the harmful act. Perhaps we should apply this view to those people who are conventionally

禪

labeled as evil. Such people definitely need to be restrained for the safety of others and given the help they need to lead more constructive and healthy lives, but they, too, have Buddha-nature and should be regarded with equanimity and treated with respect. A similar attitude can help us respond without prejudice and hostility to those who are unattractive or displeasing to us in some more minor way.

As we follow the Buddhist path, we may at times fall prey to indolence and allow ourselves to become distracted by activities that impede our progress on the path. We may also occasionally harbor feelings of discouragement and self-contempt. *Determination* is the antidote to these failings, as it helps us develop and maintain enthusiasm about the path. On an everyday level, determination encourages us to reflect on the life of the Buddha and the great saints and to read inspirational texts. These activities and other religious practices, such as reciting prayers, going on pilgrimages to holy places, and making offerings to the Buddhas and bodhisattvas can help rekindle our ardor and see us through times of hardship and disappointment we may experience.

Finally, Bodhidharma taught that a seeker on the path should cultivate *insight*. Our understanding of the Dharma may begin on an intellectual level, but as we progress on the path, true insight is developed as a byproduct of meditation. The most important insight to be cultivated is a perception of the true nature of reality. This insight can lead eventually to Enlighten-

ment itself. The process of gaining insight begins quite simply, for we all have some degree of understanding. First, we study and learn about the Mahayana path. In contrast to certain later Zen masters, Bodhidharma does not seem to have discouraged the study of Buddhist teachings through its scriptures. Next, we ponder and reflect deeply on the significance of what we have learned, until we gain a deeper level of insight. Finally, we focus on what we have understood during meditation until our mind mixes with the insight and it becomes a living experience.

LESSON *Tranquility Meditation*

Bodhidharma also taught an entry to the path through meditation. Contrary to the impression given by later Zen accounts of Bodhidharma, the meditation that he taught was not especially revolutionary. Rather, his approach was innovative in that he taught meditation in China at a time when less demanding forms of spiritual practice, such as giving alms, chanting texts, or copying sutras, were in vogue.

Bodhidharma did teach a special meditation technique called "wall gazing," intended to free the mind from concepts. While this technique could work well for a meditator with some previous experience and practicing under guidance of a teacher, it is not a method suitable for beginners. If someone new to meditation came to Bodhidharma, we can assume that he might have initially taught one of the more basic methods of Buddhist meditation, such as tranquility meditation.

Tranquility meditation is designed to calm the mind and the body through focusing single-pointedly upon some appropriate object. You might focus on an image, such as a mental picture of the Buddha or, more commonly, you can focus on the breath. A few preliminaries can help ensure a fruitful meditation session.

First, choose a good place to meditate. Though it is possible to meditate anywhere, beginners should find a place where they are unlikely to be disturbed by noise from outside or from other parts of the house. The light should be dim, neither too bright nor too dark. If the space is too bright, the clarity of the room's contents can be distracting; while a dark room is more conducive to sleep than to concentration. On a low table, you might place an image of the Buddha or some other holy person, along with flowers and a receptacle for burning incense. As well as creating a pleasant fragrance, incense is calming to the senses and creates an atmosphere conducive to meditation.

Various times of the day are traditionally prescribed as most suitable for meditation, such as dawn, dusk, and midnight, though people with busy working lives may not be able to adopt these times for practice. The most important thing is to fix a time that is best for you and stick to that. Changing your time for meditation every day is not conducive to regular practice, since you soon begin to find reasons why your schedule makes it impossible to do any meditation that day! It is also advisable to limit yourself to sessions of no more than thirty minutes.

The question of the best meditation posture for Westerners is open to argument. Some forms of Buddhism are quite relaxed about posture, but the Zen tradition, especially Japanese Zen, lays great stress on a formal, traditional posture. They prescribe that meditators sit with the legs locked in the full "lotus pose," in which the soles are upturned and placed on top of the opposite thighs. Many meditators cannot adopt this position without pain, which would seem to defeat the whole object of meditating to calm the mind! A compromise is to sit in a more relaxed

禪

"tailor posture," with the legs bent and folded in front. Sitting on a small thick cushion or a meditation stool that elevates the back will help you fold your legs more easily. It is also possible to meditate sitting upright in a chair, with your feet placed flat on the ground. Your hands should be placed palms upwards, one on top of the other, with the tips of the thumbs raised and touching to form a circle. Your shoulders should be relaxed, but your back should be held straight and upright without strain, and your head very slightly inclined forward. Your eyes should be half-closed, with your gaze directed downwards to a point about four feet in front of you. When you first sit down to meditate, spend a few minutes getting comfortable so that you feel balanced and relaxed. Breathe in and out deeply several times.

The object of tranquility meditation is focusing the mind without distraction. The easiest object of focus is the breathing process itself. It is not necessary to alter your breathing as one might in some forms of yoga. Rather, when you are sufficiently relaxed, turn your attention to the flow of your breath, focusing on the point above your upper lip where the breath enters and leaves your nostrils. Some instructions suggest that you count each cycle of inhalation and exhalation, beginning with one and counting up to ten cycles. Counting is a means of strengthening the mind's focus on the breathing.

When your mind wanders away from the breathing cycle, as it surely will, gently bring it back to focus on the breathing as soon as you notice it has drifted off target. Do not become annoyed with yourself, for it is quite natural for beginners to lose their focus. Instead, just resume counting the inward and outward flow of your breath. As you make progress with this form of meditation, you may notice that your breathing becomes slower and increasingly subtle. By the time you have reached this stage, you will be able to focus on the breathing without any further need for counting.

When you have finished your meditation session, do not suddenly jump up and rush off into the turmoil of your daily life. Buddhists believe that any wholesome activity, such as meditation, generates a charge of positive energy. This energy can be shared with others for their benefit. Consequently, at the end of your meditation session, you might express your desire that the positive energy you have accumulated through practice might be transferred to others.

The simple instructions given here can help you get started on a meditation practice. It's important to remember, however, that meditation is a powerful tool for change. Because it acts upon the mind, it may bring up complex emotions and long-forgotten or suppressed memories. Thus it is a good idea to seek out a Buddhist group or arrange for access to a qualified meditation teacher who can advise and encourage you appropriately as you venture into the unknown and sometimes disturbing territory that is your own mind.

禅

Jianzhi Sengcan *(?-606)*

The Way is not difficult for
those without preferences.

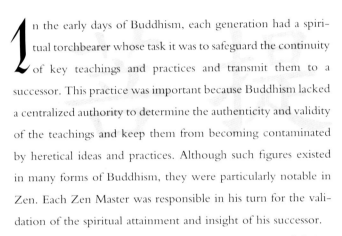

In the early days of Buddhism, each generation had a spiritual torchbearer whose task it was to safeguard the continuity of key teachings and practices and transmit them to a successor. This practice was important because Buddhism lacked a centralized authority to determine the authenticity and validity of the teachings and keep them from becoming contaminated by heretical ideas and practices. Although such figures existed in many forms of Buddhism, they were particularly notable in Zen. Each Zen Master was responsible in his turn for the validation of the spiritual attainment and insight of his successor.

As we have noted, Bodhidharma was the twenty-eighth in a line of mythical Indian patriarchs stretching back to Buddha Shakyamuni himself, thus guaranteeing the credentials of the Zen approach. Bodhidharma is also the first patriarch of Chinese Zen, since it was he who brought Zen to China. This patriarchal system was continued for several generations after Bodhidharma's death, since Zen was still a unified movement during its early days. However, during and after the time of the sixth Chinese patriarch, Huineng, the Zen movement broke up into several schools. However, the master at the head of each branch continued to validate and approve the spiritual achievements of those in his care.

As we have seen, Bodhidharma passed the patriarchal insignia and authority to teach to Huike (487-593), second patriarch of Zen in China. After Bodhidharma's death, Huike seems to have spent time at the Shaolin Monastery, though he was forced on several occasions to go into hiding in the mountains because of the persecutions that rocked the Buddhist world in China during his lifetime.

While Huike was in residence at Shaolin, a mysterious young man, possibly still a teenager, arrived at the temple. The young man gave neither his name nor his birthplace as good Chinese etiquette required. He simply asked for help since he was ill. Early Zen records tell us that he was suffering from a disease called "*feng-yang*," understood by some to mean leprosy, but more likely a form of psychological disturbance. Though Chinese medical knowledge was quite advanced at this time, many ordinary people thought that illness was a consequence of sin.

Knowing that Huike was a master of high spiritual ability, the young man approached Huike and asked him to accept his repentance and absolve him from his sins, believing that this absolution would cure his illness. We can imagine the young man kneeling before Huike and making his request with a humble bow.

Huike's reply was unexpected and enigmatic. "Bring me your sins, and I'll absolve you," he told the young man.

The young man paused for a few moments. Then he said softly, "I've searched for them, but I can't find them anywhere!"

Huike's reply was kind but direct. "Then I now absolve you. Take refuge in the Buddha, the Dharma, and the Sangha." With that, perhaps he expected that the young man would go on his

禅

way satisfied. But as is often the case in Zen conversations, the dialogue between master and student moved to a different level of understanding.

The young man explained to Huike that he understood that the Sangha was the community of monks, but he wondered about the meaning of the Buddha and the Dharma.

Huike answered cautiously. "The heart-mind is the Buddha; the heart-mind is the Dharma. There is no difference between Buddha, the teacher, and Dharma, the teachings. Do you understand?"

The young man paused again. Suddenly a light began to shine from his face. "Ah! Now I understand! Sins have no reality, neither internally or externally. Since my heart-mind is free from sin, it is identical to the Buddha and the Dharma!"

Impressed by this degree of insight, Huike recognized that the young man had great potential and accepted him into the monastery, bestowing upon him the name *Sengcan* ("treasure of the community") since he was like a jewel to the Sangha. It is recorded that Sengcan served Huike for six years, even accompanying him into the mountains during the great persecution of 574.

When that troubled time had passed, Sengcan parted from Huike, but not before he had been given the patriarchal tokens that made him the third Zen patriarch in China. Though some fragmentary anecdotes survive, the remainder of Sengcan's life is as mysterious as his early years, though he is known to have died in 606. The epitaph from his tomb praises him highly for his friendliness, gentleness, and detachment from the world.

禅

TEACHINGS *The Mind*

Like many scholars and teachers of the vibrant and creative Sui and Tang eras, Sengcan and other early Zen Masters, having thoroughly assimilated the Buddha's message, set out to recast the Buddha's teachings in ways that appealed to the Chinese mind. Chinese thought differed fundamentally from Indian ways of thinking in many respects. For example, Indian Buddhists relied on a wide range of textual materials and tended to be rather long-winded at times, whereas Chinese and later Japanese Buddhists often focused on a particular sutra that seemed to epitomize their understanding of Buddhism. Some even abandoned scriptural study altogether. Frequently, the teachings of a single sutra were adopted as the doctrinal basis for a new school of Buddhism.

For many Zen Buddhists of Sengcan's time, the sutra that was chosen as a focus was the Lankavatara Sutra, a complex Mahayana scripture said to recount the teachings given by the Buddha when he visited Sri Lanka. It was believed that Bodhidharma himself especially esteemed this work and included his oral instructions on it as part of his transmission to Huike. Sengcan, in turn, is known to have lectured on the Lankavatara Sutra during his teaching career.

The appeal of the Lankavatara Sutra for Zen followers is obvious. Although it covers a wide range of topics, its central theme is the nature of the mind and its relationship to reality.

The Lankavatara Sutra teaches that everything that we normally experience in the world is a delusion; in other words, nothing exists in the way it appears to our mind. The Buddha taught that as a result of spiritual ignorance, our ordinary mind creates a split between the self that perceives the world and the objects that the mind perceives. However, this perception of duality is a delusion, no more real than the images that appear to the mind in dreams. Moreover, seeing the world in this deluded way does not reflect the intrinsic state of the mind, which the Lankavatara Sutra teaches is pure and inherently enlightened. This inherently enlightened mind, characterized by total freedom from all discriminating conceptual thought, delusions, and negative emotions, is called Buddha-nature, the "heart-mind" that underlies the dialogue between Huike and Sengcan.

This concern with the nature of the mind is reflected in the short verse work known as the Memorial on Trust in the Heart-Mind (*Xin-xin-ming*), usually attributed to Sengcan. In fewer than 650 characters, this work summarizes the key spiritual concerns of Zen Buddhism. In it, Sengcan repeatedly stresses that speculative conversations and other activities that encourage value judgments based on our likes and dislikes may be harmful, for such habits serve to strengthen our separation from the primordial state of mind, which is Enlightenment. Thus Sengcan emphasizes a central teaching of Zen Buddhism: Enlightenment is at hand for all people if only they cut through the delusion of

禪

dualistic thinking. When Huike identified the Buddha, the Dharma, and the Sangha with the heart-mind that is Buddha-nature, he was indicating that the source of the Buddha in the world is just this Buddha-nature, that the Dharma is its verbal expression, and that the Sangha exists in the world as a result of the reality of Buddha-nature. Though Sengcan seemed to rely on meditation and other conventional techniques to achieve the goal of Enlightenment, many of the later Zen Masters who we shall encounter in this book employed increasingly innovative and radical measures to achieve this conceptual breakthrough.

禪

LESSON *A Lecture from Sengcan*

We know from surviving Zen chronicles that Sengcan used to lecture on his Xin-xin-ming to appreciative groups of students. Let's take a selection of key lines from Sengcan's poem and try to recreate the kind of teachings he might have given.

The Memorial on Trust in the Heart-Mind opens with a verse that summarizes succinctly the message of the entire work:

The ultimate way is not difficult—it just disdains selectivity;
If you just stop rejection and attachment, you will penetrate its lucidity.

You have all come here today because you are sincere seekers after truth. Some of you will have traveled the country, visiting famous masters in the hope of gaining insight into the Buddha's message, and perhaps your failure to do so has resulted in a sense of defeat. But I want to stress that the way to Enlightenment is not difficult. We just make it difficult because of the way we approach it. Enlightenment is a state of nonduality. It requires that you leave behind your speculation and your habitual value judgments about success and failure, for these only strengthen your habit of dualistic thinking. To the enlightened mind, there is no division between truth and falsehood, between what you accept and what you reject, between victory and defeat, between self and other.

Stop pursuing the objects of perception, don't dwell in emptiness;
Be patient and calmly balanced in oneness and confusion will vanish by itself.

Ordinary people who have not had much contact with the Dharma get very involved in the objects around them because these things seem so real and solid. Yet materialism is doomed to failure, since all things are impermanent, and their loss inevitably causes distress. Other people have cultivated the profound Buddhist teaching of emptiness, denying the world in an attempt to see everything as illusory. But this path of negation does not work either, as it only generates a false sense of peace. The balanced approach is the Middle Way, neither accepting nor rejecting anything you experience. Try to remain in a state of calm equipoise without making judgments, without going to extremes. Then things will become clear to you, and the natural state of your mind will shine forth.

禪

Too much talking and too much thinking makes you incapable;

Cease talking and cease thinking, then there is nowhere you cannot reach.

Most people find it very difficult to overcome the belief that by talking and thinking incessantly about truth, they can somehow grasp it. In fact, the opposite is true. Too much talking and thought creates the illusion of seeking truth, as these activities seem easier than actually doing something truthful. We all have opinions, but what use are they to us? Have you noticed that the truly wise tend to talk very little? As the Daoists say, "Those who know do not speak; those who speak do not know." Actually, the more we talk and think about truth, the further we are from it, for the simple reason that truth transcends words and thoughts.

Grasping it results in loss of freedom and the mind enters false paths;

Letting go of it results in the natural state, its essence neither leaving nor abiding.

When we think and talk, we make judgments. Based on those judgments—what we think is this and not that, good and not bad—we set goals for ourselves. In the context of the spiritual quest, the worst thing we can do is to try to grasp the nature of truth through concepts. This grasping only confuses us. Live, rather, in the here and now, not making judgments, but doing what needs to be done with mindfulness.

The believing mind is nondual and nonduality is the believing mind;

Where there are words, the way is impeded, for it is neither past, present, nor future.

All this is not easy. We are so used to making judgments that we may feel a deep sense of disquiet when we cease habitual activity. You may be wondering, Is it really possible to live without grasping for what seems to be true and important? But I say to you, only develop trust and the way will become clear. Trust that everything will turn out well, and that if you let go of the habits of a lifetime, the true way will manifest itself, for it has always been present. By your frantic efforts to think your way to Enlightenment, you have been blocking the truth that Enlightenment is the natural state of your own mind, beyond all divisions of past, present, and future.

禪

Dajian Huineng *(638-713)*

Confused by thoughts,
we experience duality in life.
Unencumbered by ideas,
the enlightened see the one Reality.

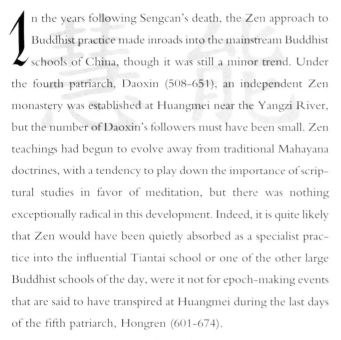

In the years following Sengcan's death, the Zen approach to Buddhist practice made inroads into the mainstream Buddhist schools of China, though it was still a minor trend. Under the fourth patriarch, Daoxin (508-651), an independent Zen monastery was established at Huangmei near the Yangzi River, but the number of Daoxin's followers must have been small. Zen teachings had begun to evolve away from traditional Mahayana doctrines, with a tendency to play down the importance of scriptural studies in favor of meditation, but there was nothing exceptionally radical in this development. Indeed, it is quite likely that Zen would have been quietly absorbed as a specialist practice into the influential Tiantai school or one of the other large Buddhist schools of the day, were it not for epoch-making events that are said to have transpired at Huangmei during the last days of the fifth patriarch, Hongren (601-674).

Huineng, a poor man in his early thirties, had been selling firewood to support himself and his widowed mother in the backwaters of southern China. One day, he heard by chance somebody chanting a passage from the Diamond Sutra. When he heard the line, "Let your mind flow freely without dwelling on anything," he had a sudden yet disturbing experience of awakening. Though illiterate, he realized that he needed to find a teacher who could give him further instructions. He wandered around the countryside for a few years visiting various monasteries, no doubt widening his knowledge of Buddhist doctrines

and practices. Finally, he ended up at Huangmei, Hongren's monastery. Because Huineng was a layman, it was improper for him to join the monks formally. But his earnest request for instruction obviously made an impression on Hongren, who offered him a position as a menial worker hulling rice in the kitchen for the community.

By now, Hongren was an old man. Knowing that he would soon die, he announced a contest to select his successor. Anyone who wished to put himself forward as a candidate was to compose a short poem of realization expressing his insights into Buddhism and post it on a wall of the monastery. One of Hongren's students, the learned and highly respected Shenxiu (605?-706), was expected by all to win, so nobody else bothered to compete. The poem that Shenxiu wrote, with modest reservations about his abilities, was a profound statement of the type of Zen that had been practiced up until that time:

> The body is like a *bodhi* tree
> And the mind a bright mirror.
> Carefully polish it clean every day,
> And let no dust alight.

When he saw the verse, Hongren had incense burned before it and praised it, saying that anybody who practiced in this way would attain Enlightenment. Later that day, Huineng asked one

禪

of the monks to read Shenxiu's poem to him. With this monk's help, Huineng had a reply written which was posted in the wall during the hours of darkness, alongside Shenxiu's composition:

From the start, there is no *bodhi* tree
Nor stand of a bright mirror.
Buddha-nature is ever pure;
Where can the dust alight?

While Shenxiu had presented an approach to Buddhist practice that works well empirically, Huineng demonstrated that he understood the Dharma more deeply. His poem makes clear that everything in this world—the tree under which the Buddha attained Enlightenment, objects such as the mirror, even the mind itself—has merely relative truth status. Buddha-nature is the ever-present, true nature of all beings. It does not need to be purified since it is intrinsically untouchable by dustlike negative thoughts and emotions. Huineng's poem suggests that, rather than the arduous practice of watching the mind to keep it clear of negative thoughts, only a radical change in perspective can reveal the pure Buddha-nature intrinsic to each being.

The monks were perplexed and wondered who had challenged Shenxiu. Yet Hongren himself knew that there was only one person at the monastery who had attained the level of

禅

accomplishment revealed by this verse: Huineng. One night soon afterwards, Hongren called Huineng to his room and bestowed upon him the symbols of the patriarchy: the robe and the bowl. Hongren realized that there would be great opposition if this illiterate outsider took his place as the sixth patriarch, so he advised Huineng to leave immediately and hide out in the south of China. Indeed, as he fled, Huineng was pursued by a group of angry monks, but he is said to have overcome their hostility by his deep understanding and powers as a teacher. Nevertheless, Huineng did not return to Hongren's monastery but instead took refuge in the mountains, where he spent some fifteen years in solitary meditation.

At the end of this self-imposed exile, Huineng was visiting the monastery of Faxin. There he heard two monks engaged in a heated philosophical debate about a flag fluttering in the wind. One monk insisted that it was the flag itself that was moving, while the other maintained that it was the wind that was moving. Huineng swiftly settled the argument, saying to them, "It is neither the flag nor the wind that moves. It is your mind that moves." Word of this wise answer reached the abbot of the monastery, who recognized that the visitor was Huineng, whose fame had reached his ears. As Huineng had never been ordained as a monk, the abbot kindly arranged for him to take his vows and to teach his understanding of Zen at the Faxin monastery.

Now nearly fifty years of age, Huineng spent the rest of his life teaching at various monasteries in the south of China, far away from the political upheavals and intrigues that had begun to tear at the heart of the Tang Empire. However, his

禪

reputation did reach the imperial court. Toward the end of his life, at a monastery near Canton, Huineng is said to have preached his famous Platform Sutra. After his death, Huineng's body was mummified and lacquered to preserve it, apparently with success, for it is enshrined in China to this day.

Meanwhile, in the north, Hongren had long since passed away, and the patriarchal lineage there was passed on, as expected, to Shenxiu. Shenxiu himself went on to become one of the most eminent and respected Buddhist figures of Tang Dynasty China, with honors showered upon him by several emperors. Although Huineng and Shenxiu were actually on good terms, the dispute about the validity of their respective methods later became quite bitter, thanks to the animosity stirred up by one of Huineng's successors, Shenhui. The schism between followers of Huineng and Shenxiu resulted in the emergence of two rival systems of Zen: the Northern School and the Southern School.

Based in the bustling urban centers around the twin capitals, Loyang and Chang'an, the Northern School still maintained many elements of the traditional Indian Mahayana approach to achieving Enlightenment. Its followers advocated continual practice through meditation, accompanied by study of key scriptures such as the Lankavatara Sutra, the Diamond Sutra, and the Flower Garland Sutra. They felt that these scriptures provided valuable insights into the dynamics of the mind and how it should be understood and trained. They also stressed the importance of conventional Buddhist morality and discipline combined with good works for the benefit of ordinary people.

The Southern School, founded by Huineng, defined itself by its belief in "the sudden approach" to Enlightenment. Following Huineng's lead, his followers discarded virtually all scholarly study of scriptures, though they did esteem the Diamond Sutra to a degree. They held that since Buddha-nature lies within everybody, Enlightenment is not to be attained through a process of acquisition or the gradual accumulation of merit and wisdom. Rather, the practitioner should seek a sudden and intuitive breakthrough that cuts through the deluding thoughts and emotions that veil the enlightened mind. Thus for the Southern School, only a direct and unmediated experience of reality can open the way to Enlightenment.

Though the Northern School survived for over two hundred years after Shenxiu's passing, it eventually withered away into oblivion. Despite much hostile criticism from Huineng's successor Shenhui and his followers, its disappearance probably had less to do with its spiritual validity than with the fact that it was closely linked to an urban society that was devastated by civil wars and invasions in the decades after Shenxiu. By contrast, Huineng's Southern School, safely isolated from these upheavals in the remote south, emerged eventually as the unique Chinese form of Buddhism that flourished and has survived down to the present day.

禅

TEACHINGS *Seeing Into One's Own Nature*

Although Zen practice and teachings prior to Huineng had taken on more and more local Chinese cultural coloring, it was with Huineng that Zen truly began to emerge out of its Indian guise. With him, Zen entered into its golden age in China. Possibly because he was said to have been an illiterate peasant, Huineng rejected book learning and other forms of scholarly erudition. Rather, his style of teaching was practical, vigorous, and down-to-earth, with a good dose of dry humor. Huineng is said to have introduced the famous phrase: "Seeing into one's own nature" (*jian-xing*). According to Huineng, this "seeing," or attaining insight into one's own Buddha-nature, could only be an instantaneous event rather than a gradual process. Such insight had implicitly been the goal of Zen Buddhism, but after Huineng, it emerged explicitly as the essence of the teachings.

Huineng's teachings, anecdotes, and lectures were recorded in a text known popularly as the Platform Sutra of the Sixth Patriarch. Recent research on this text using manuscript materials discovered in the early 1900s at the ancient Chinese border oasis outpost of Dun-huang has cast considerable doubt that Huineng himself authored the entire collection, for the text is now known to have been expanded over the centuries with additional material. In fact, it seems to reflect the views of Huineng's ambitious disciple, Shenhui, rather than those of the master himself. However, it is certain that the core of the teachings in the Platform Sutra does derive from Huineng's approach even if he did not write the manuscript himself.

The Platform Sutra can basically be divided into two portions, a sermon with an introductory autobiography given at a certain Dafan monastery and a selection of talks and instructions said to have been delivered by Huineng on other occasions. Later Zen stories emphasize Huineng's illiteracy and hostility to scriptural study, but the early Dun-huang version of the Platform Sutra leads us to think that this emphasis is an apocryphal device added later by Shenhui and his followers to proclaim the availability of Zen teachings to everyone, no matter their station in life. On the contrary, the Platform Sutra uses terminology and concepts derived from wide range of scriptures, sometimes quoted word-for-word, although they are given a particularly Zen flavor when expounded by Huineng.

The sermon itself contains several important themes. Following the opening autobiography, Huineng asserts the intrinsic identity of meditation (*dhyana*) and insight (*prajna*). Some followers of Buddhism in China believed that a practitioner needed to engage in meditative concentration in order to generate spiritual insight. But Huineng, in line with the teachings of the Nirvana Sutra, said that this was not the case. All beings, he maintained, are inherently endowed with insight, which is released simultaneously with meditation practice. In other words, meditation and insight are related like a lamp and its light. For Huineng,

that lies beyond the realm of words and concepts. Attachment to words and concepts interrupts the natural state of the mind and results in a stream of successive thoughts that lead to bondage and continued rebirth. Cutting attachment to this stream of thoughts at any one moment breaks this process and brings about the state of no-thought, the sudden breakthrough that gives one a glimpse of the enlightened state. A celebrated passage in the Platform Sutra sums up this approach:

When the sudden doctrine is understood, there is no need to discipline yourself in external things. If you always have the right view within your mind, you will never be deluded. This is seeing into your own nature.

insight seems to have been virtually equivalent to the intrinsic awareness associated with Buddha-nature.

Closely allied to this idea of inherent insight is the concept of "direct mind," an approach to meditation in which the practitioner allows the mind to rest in its natural state without attachment to anything whatsoever, even to the meditation practice itself. This view of meditation practice is linked with an important Zen concept variously known as "no-thought," "non-form," and "non-abiding." These terms seem to refer to the natural or intrinsic state of mind, which is Enlightenment, a state

Finally, despite the differences between the Southern and Northern schools, Huineng taught that there are not two different ways to attain Enlightenment. What gives rise to the two approaches is the different levels of ability among practitioners rather than any intrinsic difference in the result. Some people are better suited to the gradual path of meditation, scriptural study, discipline, and good works; while others benefit more from practicing "no thought" and from seeking a sudden breakthrough to enlightened consciousness. In other words, both methods are taught as expedient means to help beings extricate themselves from the unrelenting cycle of birth and death.

禪

LESSON *Confusion versus Insight*

Let's look at a few passages from Huineng's Platform Sutra and see what lessons they have for us today.

Underpinning the idea of sudden Enlightenment as taught by Huineng and the Southern School is the belief that Enlightenment is present in or pervades all beings. In ordinary beings, Enlightenment is merely concealed by delusion and negativity. We differ from the Buddhas only in that we are ignorant of that Enlightenment while the Buddhas are awakened to it. Huineng's views on this distinction are neatly summarized in a short passage from the Platform Sutra:

Deluded: a Buddha is an ordinary being,

Awakened: an ordinary being is a Buddha.

Confusion: a Buddha is an ordinary being,

Insight: an ordinary being is a Buddha.

Here Huineng points out that ordinary beings and Buddhas are like two sides of a coin: essentially identical, they are what they are because of how they view themselves. To paraphrase a famous Buddhist master, there is no difference between us and the Enlightened Beings except that they know they are enlightened and we do not!

Looking at ourselves in light of this teaching can be very empowering. Many religions emphasize the inherent sinfulness and corruption of human beings, a state that can be overcome only by the grace of God. How different this view is from the Buddhist position! Buddhism maintains that all beings are inherently good despite an overlay of delusion and that all evil flows from that deluded state. Thus even the most seemingly evil people whom we like to demonize are potential Buddhas. A thoughtful Buddhist condemns the evil that people do but still tries to value the person by generating thoughts of loving-kindness and compassion as part of meditation practice. The all-pervading presence of Buddha-nature in others should also remind us that even humble, insignificant people are worthy of respect. Zen practitioners often acknowledge the potential that all have for Enlightenment by bowing to each other at the end of a group meditation as they would to an image of the Buddha himself.

If the mind is corrupt, a Buddha is an ordinary being,

If the mind is balanced, an ordinary being is a Buddha.

Once a corrupted mind has arisen,

Buddhahood is hidden within ordinary beings.

In this passage, Huineng highlights the basic human dilemma: When the mind is shrouded by the corrupting power of delusion, false value judgments, and negative emotions, the intrinsic nature of the primordially enlightened mind is utterly hidden from view. What should we do about this? Huineng

禪

tells us that Buddhahood shines forth when we become "balanced." By a balanced mind, he means one that does not get involved in grasping and attachment. Attachment always creates imbalance. We take one side over another, or think that one thing is better than another thing. As Zen Masters implore us again and again: avoid attachments and just let the mind be. Even meditation itself can be an occasion for attachment. If you meditate with a goal in mind—even the goal of Enlightenment— you risk becoming attached to that goal. The ideal, difficult as it is to achieve, is to meditate as though it were as natural as breathing and sleeping.

If we are able to achieve such natural balance, even for an instant, the clouds part and delusions and discriminatory thoughts subside. Huineng refers to this breakthrough as "seeing one's nature." At this moment, the mind returns to its natural state and functions as Buddha-mind:

If for one thought-instant they become balanced,
Then ordinary beings are themselves Buddhas.
A mere taste of Buddha-mind is sufficient to change
your whole life.
Once experienced, the insight that you gain
is never lost.

Finally, Huineng teaches, never doubt your own capabilities:

The Buddha is present in our mind itself
Our own Buddha is the true Buddha.
If we ourselves are devoid of the Buddha-mind,
Then where shall we seek the Buddha?

As Huineng understood, many people have been led to believe that they are worthless, that their only hope for salvation lies outside themselves, in some deity or supernatural force, or through the help of some priest or teacher. But as Huineng tells us, we must trust ourselves.

Implicitly, Huineng invites us to examine our relationship with any spiritual guide. How do we view them? Even more importantly, how do they view us? Do they try to create dependency by trying to convince us that we cannot progress on the path without their help? Or do they empower us to rely on the guidance of our own inherent Buddha-nature? A teacher can be very helpful, but we cannot rely upon them for Enlightenment.

The same caution applies to the instruction we might get from books. Huineng and his successors criticized the way some people studied the scriptures because of the tendency to intellectualize the Dharma or to regard study as an end in itself. Buddhist texts can be very inspiring, but as the Buddha taught, they are merely a raft to cross the river.

禅

Yuquan Shenxiu *(605?-706)*

You should abide in meditation and awareness
after having achieved the contemplation of nonsubstantiality;
not abiding in being and nonbeing,
the body and the mind are identical like space.

It is often noted that it is the victors who write history. This is very true in the case of the Southern and the Northern schools of Zen, though it might be more accurate to say that the Southern School won out over the Northern by default rather than as a result of doctrinal or practical superiority. Nevertheless, for centuries our views of the Northern School founded by Shenxiu have been colored by the partisan account of its teachings given in The Platform Sutra, the text attributed to Huineng but probably partly authored by Huineng's ambitious disciple Shenhui. To do Shenxiu and the Northern School justice, we need to lay aside Shenhui's attacks and look at their ideas without preconceptions.

Judging from other accounts, Yuquan Shenxiu was a Zen Master of towering achievements. Though his story lacks some of the drama we associate with better known masters, it is remarkable in its own way. Shenxiu was born into an aristocratic family near present-day Kaifeng. Evidence suggests that his family had close connections with the Tang royal family, which makes sense given Shenxiu's close relationship with emperor Ruizong and empress Wu later in his life. As befitted a person of aristocratic birth, Shenxiu had a first-rate education, which included the Confucian classics as well as Daoist and Buddhist works.

Even as a teenager, Shenxiu seems to have had a forceful personality. When he was thirteen, a series of terrible famines and epidemics swept the provinces of Shandong and Henan. His feelings of pity aroused, Shenxiu traveled to the official granaries at Kaifeng and begged the superintendents to release grain to feed the suffering populace. While engaged in this relief work, he encountered a Buddhist monk who inspired him to become a monk himself.

After taking the precepts of a novice monk, Shenxiu traveled widely throughout China, visiting distant cities and climbing many sacred mountains on pilgrimage. In 625, when he was about twenty, he took full vows at the Tiangong Monastery near Loyang. As was usual for talented new monks, Shenxiu first studied the Vinaya and learned how to perform the various rituals and ceremonies that took place at large Buddhist monasteries. Assuming that he followed the typical program, he would have spent the next years in intensive meditation practice and scriptural study.

We next hear of Shenxiu in 651 when he was in his late forties and went to study under the fifth patriarch Hongren at Huangmei. There are no reliable reports of Shenxiu's activities during the seven years he spent there. The story told in Chapter 3 about Hongren's contest to choose a successor, in which Shenxiu's realization poem was bested by that of the newcomer Huineng, may be nothing more than a pious fiction devised by Huineng's supporters to discredit Shenxiu. Or it may be that the story is simply an effective and dramatic teaching device. Thus we can't be sure what level of spiritual attainment Shenxiu

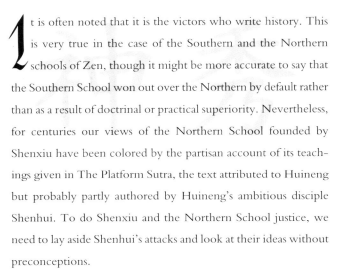

禪

reached at Huangmei, though it seems likely he was quite advanced, since his biographies tell us that Hongren praised him as a monk of the highest acumen and accorded him special attention. Nor do we know precisely when Shenxiu was officially recognized as the sixth patriarch after Hongren's death in 674.

We do know, however, that in 657, years before assuming the patriarchy, Shenxiu traveled to the capital city of Chang'an to teach Buddhism. His stay there was cut short by political events. Tang emperors were often ambivalent toward Buddhism—sometimes lavishing huge resources upon the community, other times subjecting it to restrictions or even persecution. In 662, against a backdrop of Daoist-Buddhist rivalry, emperor Gaozong announced a list of "reforms" designed to restrict the privileges traditionally enjoyed by Buddhist monks and nuns. These proclamations were greeted with protests and demonstrations by the Buddhist clergy. Given his connections with the royal family, Shenxiu may have tried to persuade

Gaozong to change his mind. Unsuccessful in this attempt, Shenxiu was forced to leave the capital and go into exile. Since Shenxiu is said to have disguised himself as a layman for many years during this period, it may be that his life was in danger.

When political tensions eased and Gaozong dropped his controversial reforms, Shenxiu returned to full monastic life. In 677, he took up residence at a monastery in Jingzhou specially allocated to him. By now he was famed as a master. Numerous students flocked to Jingzhou, "like clouds following the dragon"—so many that Shenxiu's biographies tell us that a kind of shantytown grew up around his monastery to house all those who wanted to study with him. Even Shenhui, who did so much later to destroy Shenxiu's reputation, became his student. One wonders what passed between master and pupil to cause Shenhui's later hostility. Official records show no trace of a quarrel. In fact, it seems that Shenxiu complimented Shenhui and arranged for Shenhui's teacher Huineng to be invited to the

禅

capital. Shenxiu also encouraged his students to visit Huineng "for he knows the true principles of the Dharma."

The high point of Shenxiu's career occurred when he attracted the attention of the empress Wu (624–705). This pious woman usurped the Tang throne in 690 during one of its periods of weakness and used her position to promote Buddhism with great vigor. In 701, at the invitation of the empress, Shenxiu traveled to the city of Loyang. Renowned as the greatest living Buddhist master of the day, Shenxiu was showered with ceremonial honors. In the palace chapel, empress Wu bowed to Shenxiu, an event without precedent in Chinese history. The empress confirmed Shenxiu as the sixth Zen patriarch, giving him the robe and bowl insignia said to have belonged to Bodhidharma. This imperial patronage guaranteed that the Zen approach was considered the orthodox school within Chinese Buddhism.

The last years of Shenxiu's life were spent traveling between the twin capitals of Loyang and Chang'an as empress Wu's chaplain. By the end of Shenxiu's life, the empress herself had quietly been demoted after a bloodless restoration of the legitimate Tang rulers, though the old empress still wielded considerable influence. In April 706, Shenxiu fell ill and died while sitting in meditation at the Tiangong Monastery where he had been ordained. As befitted his stature, his funeral was a lavish affair. The new emperor Zhongzong, princes, and court officials followed his body on foot before it was interred.

Thus passed a monk renowned for his great moral integrity, unbounded compassion, and penetrating intellect. It is unfortunate that Shenxiu's place in the history of Zen was lost from view for centuries through the efforts of his disgruntled ex-disciple Shenhui, who was perhaps motivated in his attacks on Shenxiu and his Northern School by a desire to have himself recognized as the seventh patriarch. It seems fitting that the side-lineage of Zen that Shenhui established died out even before the Northern School he so despised!

禪

TEACHINGS *Contemplating the Mind*

Shenxiu is important historically because he transmitted the Zen doctrines and practices he learned from the fifth patriarch Hongren at his monastery at Huangmei to people in the capital cities. Before Shenxiu's time, Huangmei had been the sole center for Zen in China. Zen history maintains that after Hongren's death, his lineage was passed on to Huineng, who was named as the sixth patriarch before being forced to flee his rivals. Recent research, however, especially that based on material found in the caves of Dunhuang, has forced scholars to reexamine the assumption that the true lineage of Zen passed to Huineng and the Southern School. From a comparison of surviving writings and several newly discovered works believed to have been written by Shenxiu, many now believe that it was he who most faithfully carried on the lineage of Hongren and his predecessors.

The teachings of Shenxiu and the Northern School may seem conventional when compared to the "sudden approach" to Enlightenment taught by the Zen Masters of the Southern School. Critics called Shenxiu's method "gradualism"—a plodding, step-by-step approach to spiritual development. However, as the new writings show, Shenxiu offered teachings that were complex, yet flexible. Information about Shenxiu's teachings comes from three literary sources: the Treatise on the Contemplation of the Mind (*Guanxin Lun*) and two short works found at Dunhuang, the Treatise of Perfect Illumination

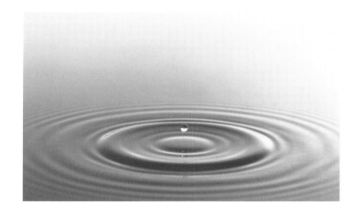

(*Yuanming Lun*) and The Five Expedient Means (*Wu Fangbian*). The works found at Dunhuang have the unpolished feel of lecture notes and so seem to provide an accurate account of Shenxiu's teaching style.

As with all Zen Masters, the role of the mind is central to Shenxiu's teachings. Thus we read in the Treatise of Perfect Illumination:

Q: If somebody seeks Enlightenment, what is the most quintessential factor that can be cultivated?

A: Only the single factor of contemplating the mind which completely encompasses all practice is quintessential . . . Of all things, the mind is fundamental; all phenomena are simply products of the mind. Therefore know that all good and evil arises from your own mind. To seek Enlightenment somewhere outside of the mind is an utter impossibility.

禅

According to Buddhism, the mind has two functions or aspects: the ultimate nature of pure mind, which we may term the mind's "suchness," and the mind's relative or conventional nature, which can be defiled by delusion and negativity. These two aspects are provisionally conjoined but not mutually dependent. In other words, both are present and functioning in us, but neither causes the other to exist. The relationship between these two aspects of mind is best shown by the metaphor of the sun and clouds. In our current unenlightened state, both the relative mind with its contents of deluded thoughts and emotions and the shining, sunlike brightness of pure mind are present. However, the sunlike pure mind is unaffected in any way by the obscuring blanket of cloudlike thoughts and emotions that pass across the relative mind.

These two aspects of mind are echoed in two levels of reality in everything that exists, one that is absolutely real and the other that is real only in a relative or conventional sense. The absolute level is the state in which the enlightened mind operates and perceives things as they are. The relative level refers to the everyday world of unenlightened beings who perceive and describe things in a distorted though convenient way. From the ultimate point of view, everything associated with the relative level is illusory. The traditional example is a person who sees a coiled shape in a dark room. Terrified that the shape is a poisonous snake, the person jumps back in fear. The light of a lamp reveals, however, that the shape is simply a piece of old rope. As this example shows, our deluded mind makes assumptions about what we see and experience. We then accept that these perceptions are "real" and "substantial" and react accordingly. The same is true of every perception of the relative mind. When the enlightened mind perceives objects, it does so without the intervening overlay of misconceptions and emotional baggage.

Since pure mind is present in us, how does the deluded mind come into being? Teachers of the Northern School explain the process this way: Because we fail to recognize the presence of the enlightened mind, or perhaps because we are afraid to trust ourselves to it, a split occurs within our consciousness. To protect our sense of individuality, we generate a series of cognitive and emotional strategies to separate us as individuals from everything that is "not us." This split causes the everyday, conventional mind to come into being as an illusory phenomenon. As we filter our perceptions of reality through the emotions and expectations of the deluded mind, we create a pseudoreality, in which we believe that objects exist as we perceive them.

The famous masters of the Southern School tended to sidestep the whole issue of the deluded mind—since it does not exist anyway!—and concentrate on the innate enlightened mind. Southern School teachers taught their students to pluck up their courage and grab the "snake" without any light in the hope that at that moment they would realize that the "snake" was actu-

禪

ally a rope and break through to an enlightened perception of reality. By contrast, Shenxiu taught his students to examine the nature and functioning of the conventional mind as a way of eliminating it. He encouraged the students to focus on the thinking process itself so as to light the lamp that reveals the illusory nature of the everyday mind and its contents.

Here is Shenxiu's method: Firstly, we should contemplate the way that thoughts seem to bubble up from the mind itself as its objects. Then, to investigate the nature of thoughts and emotions, we ask ourselves a series of questions: Where do thoughts come from? Where do they abide? Where do they go? This line of investigation is designed to give us insight into the illusory nature of thoughts, the object portion of cognitive experiences.

When we have realized that thoughts—the mental representations of external objects—are illusory, the next phase of the process involves demolishing any idea we may have of the reality of the mind itself. To search for mind, we ask ourselves a second series of questions: Where is mind located? Does it exist in the past or the future? Does it have a particular form, shape, or size?

In the course of intensive meditation, we come to realize that though the everyday mind may be filled with transitory and illusory thoughts and emotions, even the mind that contains these delusions does not exist at all in an absolute sense. If we can successfully maintain our contemplation of mind at all times throughout the day, no matter what we are doing, we come to realize that the second nature of mind, its pure suchness, has been concealed under these delusions. When we glimpse this mind, identical to our Buddha-nature, awakening occurs.

This method of using step-by-step meditative analysis to break through to the absolute nature of mind does seem to be a gradual approach to Enlightenment as Shenxiu's critics charged. However, it is nonsense to claim that realization can occur without prior preparation or many years of arduous practice. In that sense, all Zen approaches are gradual. Some traditional forms of Buddhism taught that Enlightenment was gradually acquired, but all of the Zen masters—including Shenxiu—believed that Enlightenment happened suddenly. He did not instruct people to rid themselves progressively of delusions and negativity. Rather, he taught, as soon as the defiled mind is eliminated by direct insight into its nature, its delusory and negative manifestations also disappear.

But Shenxiu does differ from many later Zen Masters in China in recommending that people maintain themselves constantly in a state of awareness of the nonduality of the relative and absolute aspects of reality, of suchness and its manifestations, even after the breakthrough of awakening has occurred. Shenxiu believed that such a state of awareness was the most spiritually useful way of functioning in the world in order to benefit other beings. The goal of spiritual practice for Shenxiu was not just personal liberation but the transformation of one's small personal world into one that is great and all-encompassing.

禪

LESSON *Seeing Life as a Dream*

Shenxiu has many lessons to teach, but his message is well summed up thus:

You should abide in meditation and awareness after having achieved the contemplation of nonsubstantiality; not abiding in being and nonbeing, the body and the mind are identical like space. Ceaselessly while walking, standing, sitting, or lying down, you should try to liberate beings whenever possible. Saving the weak and helping those who have fallen low, having pity for the poor and love for the aged, you should think of the suffering of beings within the three lower modes of existence and the difficulties of the poor among humans. You should always act tirelessly to help them, even if you lose your life in the attempt.

The meditative method taught by Shenxiu may sound difficult, but it is actually a very effective and speedy way of deconstructing the everyday mind of delusion and discrimination. That everyday mind blocks our ability ceaselessly to help other beings. The main point of the method is to develop the habit of watching the mind itself—not to get involved in the thinking process, but simply to observe it and to question the apparent "reality" and "solidity" of your thoughts and feelings. It is not always necessary to verbalize the questions Shenxiu suggests about how thoughts arise and disappear, though asking these questions during formal meditation helps to develop your awareness. Rather, Shenxiu is suggesting that you maintain this awareness of your thinking process throughout the day as much as possible.

When you notice that a train of thoughts and feelings is starting to carry you away, remind yourself that thoughts have no intrinsic reality. Though they seem real, they are illusory, just like events that take place in dreams. Call to mind that no matter how dramatic, pleasant, or frightening are the events in a dream, nothing that happens is real beyond the dream itself. All dream images have been generated by your sleeping mind. The same is true of the waking reality that the mind constructs. It, too, is a dreamlike product of mind. Viewing everyday experiences as though they are dream images is a very powerful method of breaking through the sense that things and experiences exist independently of the perceiving mind. Once the objects generated by the mind have been seen for what they are—mental projections created by the everyday deluded mind—then you can start questioning the reality of that deluded, discriminating mind itself.

The goal of maintaining awareness of mind and its objects is to come to realize that both the objects generated by mind and the mind itself do not exist in the substantial and independent way you once believed. Based on this realization, Shenxiu says, you strive to maintain a mental state free from dualistic categories such as "being and nonbeing." In this state, it becomes clear that both the body as a channel for sensory experience and

禪

the mind are like space. Both lack any substantial existence. Free from the bondage of your own deluded perceptions and from any sense of limitation, you can tirelessly engage in any deeds that are necessary to help others and to guide them to liberation. This is the true purpose of Enlightenment, to act compassionately so that others might also be freed from suffering.

禪

Yixing *(685-727)*

Gone, gone, gone beyond, gone
completely beyond Enlightenment!

Yixing was one of the greatest monks of the Tang Dynasty. Despite a good grounding in the doctrines and practices of the Northern School, he is seldom mentioned in the context of Zen, perhaps because his spiritual quest led him to become involved in several other schools of Buddhism during his career. From his early years in Henan Province, Yixing devoted his life to study. He was noted as a prodigy with phenomenal powers of memory. Records say that once he had read a book, he would never have to reread it, as its contents were locked in his memory. Later in his life, he was asked by the Chinese emperor to demonstrate this gift and astonished all present at court by reciting several complete volumes of texts.

Yixing had become a monk at the age of twenty-one after the sudden loss of his parents. His first teacher was Shenxui's successor Puji (651-739), with whom he studied and meditated for several years. Following this period, Yixing studied under Huizhen (673-751), devoting his attention to a detailed study of the *Vinaya*, the rules and moral code governing the life of Buddhist monks. Later, he studied with several outstanding Tiantai Masters. By his early thirties, Yixing had come to the attention of the Imperial Court where he was renowned both as a monk and as a great mathematician and astronomer. In his role as a scientist, Yixing compiled official calendars based on the accurate observation and measurement of astronomical phenomena. He also constructed an armillary sphere, a scientific model of the celestial globe showing the orbits of the planets that combined several of the mechanical features found in present-day clocks.

While residing in Chang'an, Yixing encountered a radically new form of Buddhism that must have aroused his curiosity. From 716 onwards, Chang'an was home to a small group of Indian monks who had come to China to introduce the scriptures and practices of esoteric or Tantric Buddhism then newly developing in India. Though it did not ultimately flourish for long in China, this form of Tantric Buddhism later became extremely influential in Japan from the ninth century onwards. Yixing was initiated into these secret doctrines first by Vajrabodhi (671–741) and then by the venerable Shubhakarasimha (637–735), whose student and assistant he became. With Shubhakarasimha, Yixing translated the Mahavairocana Sutra, one of the key scriptures of esoteric Buddhism, from Sanskrit into Chinese. More importantly, he recorded Shubhakarasimha's oral commentary on this sutra in twenty volumes, a work that is still essential reading for an understanding of this important text.

Yixing's prodigious memory and devoted scholarship might have led him to even greater heights of achievement if his life had not been tragically cut short. He died at forty-two after a sudden illness. At the time of Yixing's death, his Indian teacher Shubhakarasimha was already in his nineties.

禅

TEACHINGS *The Mirror and the Sun*

Though Yixing did not live long enough to have students who would hand down his sayings and teachings, we can see traces of his Zen interests in the commentary on the Mahavairocana Sutra that he composed jointly with Shubhakarasimha. Though the bulk of this work derives from Shubhakarasimha's oral comments, Yixing also includes explanations of his own, carefully slanted to a Chinese audience as yet unfamiliar with sophisticated esoteric Buddhist doctrines.

One such contribution is his explanation of the name *Vairocana*. One of five principal manifestations of the Buddha's energy, Vairocana is called "the Illuminating Buddha." His being is symbolized by the sun. As did the Zen Masters, esoteric Buddhism teaches that Buddha-mind or Enlightenment lies within all beings and may be realized during this very lifetime if the obscuring veil of negative emotions and thoughts can be eliminated. As we have seen, Zen Masters such as Shenxiu and Huineng used the metaphor of the mirror to represent the clear Buddha-mind that is inherent in each person. Though that mirror can be obscured by dust, meditative practice and mindful vigilance can wipe the dust away. In Zen writings of the Northern School, the image of the sun has a similar meaning. Though the sun can be hidden by clouds of negativity and delusion, these obstacles can be blown away, allowing the full radiance of the inherent Buddha-mind to shine forth.

These two images—the mirror and the sun—represent two aspects of Buddha-mind: envisioned as a mirror, Buddha-mind is static, unattached to superficial phenomena; envisioned as the sun, Buddha-mind is dynamic, shining forth and illuminating reality with the light of awareness. As Yixing's commentary reminds us, we must focus our attention on the brilliant sun of Buddha-mind, symbolized by Vairocana Buddha, rather than on the distractions of obscuring ignorance and negative emotions that cloud its radiance.

禪

LESSON *Reciting Mantras*

Apart from the use of similar symbolic imagery, Zen and esoteric Buddhism have more in common than one might think at first glance. Both share a strong belief in the possibility of achieving Enlightenment in the present lifetime. Both stress the importance of a direct personal transmission of Buddha's wisdom from an accomplished master. Certain remarkable similarities can also be seen in the meditation techniques practiced by these two schools.

Zen Masters are famous for assigning their students to meditate on a kind of insoluble mind puzzle known as a *koan*. Though it seems on the surface to be quite different, the recitation of a *mantra*, a verbal formula associated with some aspect of universal Buddha-mind, a practice common in esoteric Buddhism, serves a similar purpose. The literal meaning of a mantra is less important than the way it acts as a channel opening us to our inherent Buddha-nature. The same is true of a koan, whose meaning or answer is obscure at best. Both techniques serve to shut down the discursive mind with its negative emotions and thoughts so that the radiance of the Illuminating Buddha, Vairocana, can be revealed.

Like other Zen Masters of the Tang Dynasty, Yixing was a free-thinking seeker who borrowed methods and doctrines, ideas, and techniques from other forms of Buddhism as he saw fit. From his contact with his Indian teachers Vajrabodhi and Shubhakarasimha, Yixing would have learned about mantra recitation. Let us look at two mantra practices with which Yixing would have been familiar, both of which have been used by later Zen practitioners down to modern times.

The most basic mantra is the letter sound "A" (pronounced "Ah") which Buddhist masters have taught is a manifestation of the "unborn nature of phenomena"—in other words, Enlightenment itself. The way to use this mantra in meditation practice is quite simple. After settling yourself comfortably in a meditation posture, focus on your breathing for a short time by counting the cycles of inhalation and exhalation as you have learned. Then quietly intone the sound "Ah" to yourself, excluding all other thoughts from your mind. If you shut your eyes while you are doing this, you can also try to visualize the essence of this sound in the form of a radiant bead of white light within your mind. As you become more familiar with this technique, you can stop reciting the "Ah" sound aloud and just let its sound reverberate within your mind while maintaining the image of a brilliantly shining white bead of light. Though simple, this technique is very powerful. For this reason, I recommend

禪

that you consult a reliable teacher if you want to progress further using this method as it can cause undesirable effects on the unwary.

When we meditate for a long time at a stretch, we tend to get tired, and our minds wander easily. Later Zen Masters devised various ways of dealing with such obstacles, such as alternating periods of sitting with periods of walking meditation. People engaged in the practices of esoteric Buddhism are just as likely to grow tired and careless when they meditate for a long time. Traditionally they refresh and invigorate themselves using a different method, reciting mantras aloud without any accompanying visualization. You might try using a mantra in this way. The mantra I suggest is the one included in the famous Heart Sutra, a text that speaks in koan-like terms about the process of "going beyond" our normal habits of thinking about the world.

Here is what you do: When you notice that your meditative concentration has begun to wane, open your eyes and relax a little, perhaps unfolding your legs and resting your hands on your knees. Then begin to recite the mantra, saying it aloud. If you have a set of counting beads, you can use these to keep a tally of how many times you have repeated the mantra. I suggest a minimum of 108 times, which is one round on most strings of counting beads.

Here is the mantra:

OM GATE GATE PARAGATE PARASAMGATE BODHI SVAHA

The Sanskrit words are pronounced as follows: The OM is said with the "m" sound coming through the nose, somewhat like the French sound "on." GATE, whether alone or as part of a longer word, is pronounced "gah-tay." BODHI is pronounced "bo-dee." The last word, SVAHA, is pronounced "swah-ha."

Though, as we have said, the meaning of a mantra is less important than its sound and energy, this mantra is thought to be a summation of the process leading to Enlightenment. It begins and ends with the untranslatable syllables OM and SVAHA, which open and close many mantras. In Sanskrit, GATE literally means "gone," but it also means "realize" or "understand." BODHI means "enlightenment."

Thus the Heart Sutra mantra is popularly translated "Gone, gone, gone beyond, gone completely beyond, Enlightenment!" In other words, attain illumination by realizing or understanding your own inherent Buddha-mind.

禅

Mazu Daoyi *(709-788)*

What is basically present here and now:
It does not depend on cultivating the path
or sitting in meditation.

The Golden Age of Zen in China is often said to have been inaugurated in the latter part of the eighth century CE by Mazu Daoyi. Born near Chendu in remote Sichuan, his first encounter with Zen training came when he became a monk and studied under a teacher affiliated with the fifth patriarch, Hongren. Later he moved on to Mount Heng, the home of Nanyue Huairang, a direct disciple of Huineng, the illiterate student Hongren selected to be the sixth patriarch (*see page 30*).

Some time after Mazu had settled at Mount Heng, Nanyue realized that his new student had great potential but had not quite grasped the true Zen understanding of meditation. One day, they had an exchange that has become quite famous. Their conversation has echoes of the verse Huineng had written to answer the conventional wisdom of Shenxiu's realization poem.

While Mazu was sitting in meditation, Nanyue approached him and asked casually, "What exactly is your intention by sitting all the time in meditation?"

Mazu replied laudably that he intended to become a Buddha, to become enlightened.

Without saying anything further, Nanyue picked up a piece of tile from the ground and began rubbing it on a stone.

Now it was Mazu's turn to ask a question. "What exactly is your intention by rubbing that piece of tile?"

"I'm polishing it to make a mirror," said Nanyue.

"But how can you make a mirror from a tile by grinding it on a rock?" asked a puzzled Mazu.

"How can you become a Buddha by sitting in meditation?" retorted Nanyue.

Confused, Mazu confessed his ignorance about the correct way to meditate. Nanyue then gave him instruction in how to practice "formless meditation," a spontaneous style of meditation in which the mind does not grasp at the transitory forms that arise in one's perception and thus transcends conventional ideas about good and evil. At the end of this encounter, Mazu experienced a burst of awakening. He lived with Nayue for ten more years, deepening his meditative realizations.

Later, with Nanyue's blessings, Mazu took to the road as a wandering monk and traveled throughout China, finally settling in Zhongling, where he taught the innovative nonverbal techniques that were to become the hallmark of later Zen Masters.

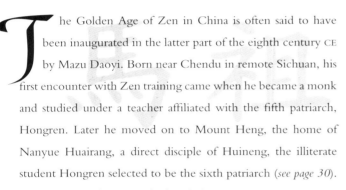

禅

TEACHINGS *Shouts and Blows*

Until Mazu entered the scene, Zen training was an austere but sedate spiritual path consisting of inspirational lectures and intense meditation. When Mazu became a Zen Master, all that began to change. Though clearly an educated man, Mazu preferred to use strident nonverbal methods to jolt his students out of their rut of preconceptions. He particularly favored striking them with his staff, shouting at them at the top of his voice, or even twisting their noses, a method brought to perfection a couple of generations later by Linji, his lineal descendent. Such behavior must have been quite terrifying for unsuspecting students, especially since Mazu had a striking physical presence. His biography states that he "strode like an ox and glared like a tiger"!

This use of violence may seem repulsive or even un-Buddhist to people who are familiar with the gentleness of teachers in others forms of Buddhism. However, Chinese society at this time had a different view of such actions. The times were violent, students were unruly, and corporal punishment was commonly used by teachers and magistrates. These factors may go some way in justifying Mazu's behavior, but shouts and blows can be useful to spiritual growth for another reason.

Zen teachings stress repeatedly that Buddha-nature is immanent, concealed just below the clouded surface of our body-mind. Any sudden shock to the body, such as a loud shout or a blow, can have the effect of cutting through the obscuring stream of conceptual thoughts and emotions for a few moments, perhaps long enough for us to glimpse the ever-present possibility of awakening. We can get some taste of this effect when somebody jumps out and gives us a fright. We move immediately to a higher level of alertness and react without any intervening conceptual thought. For a second, we just *are*—right in the midst of reality.

Mazu's use of violence can thus be seen as an unorthodox yet quite valid spiritual catalyst that aimed to give his students an experience of their true minds, their inherent Buddha-nature.

禪

LESSON *The Path of No Path*

As shouts and blows may not be a comfortable part of the spiritual path for many of us, let's look at some of Mazu's words. As we'll see, his lectures were probably as shocking to his students as his physical methods.

It is recorded that Mazu said:

What is basically present is present here and now: It does not depend on cultivating the path or sitting in meditation. Not to cultivate and not to sit, that is the pure meditation of the Buddha.

Like Mazu's students, many of us probably think of the spiritual path as a long journey toward a distant goal of spiritual awakening that can be achieved only after decades, if not lifetimes of practice and study. In most learning situations, we are accustomed to following a program of graduated steps aimed toward some achievement, some set of skills and abilities that we did not have before. But Mazu tells us here that our intrinsic Buddha-mind is not something we need to strive to realize. In fact, he implies, goal-orientated practices such as cultivating the Buddhist path or meditation are not necessary. Not only are such activities irrelevant, but they may actually hinder our realization of the pure meditation that is Enlightenment.

How can this be so? As Mazu implies, cultivating the path or sitting meditation can become subtle forms of attachment that further obscure our innate Buddha-mind. Thus any activity that we engage in on the spiritual path must be practiced without any expectation as to outcome. Sitting in meditation must be an end in itself: the path of no path and no goal.

This is how Mazu explained the path to awakening:

There is no need to cultivate the path; only do not become defiled. What is it to become defiled? A mind that discriminates life and death, and the performance of deliberate actions, is defilement. If you wish to understand the path, the ordinary mind is the path. What is called the ordinary mind? It is to be without deliberate actions, without distinguishing right and wrong, grasping and rejecting, or ordinary and holy.

Expanding on the theme of cultivating the path by not cultivating it, Mazu warns us not to let our minds become defiled by discriminations between apparent opposites—right and wrong, ordinary and holy. Such categories enmesh us in the cycle of life and death. In effect, Mazu is advising us to let go of all value judgments and preconceptions about our spiritual situation. Rather than acting with considered deliberation, we should let go and act spontaneously, for our ordinary mind is actually our Buddha-nature. If we can trust ourselves to live without deliberate actions—to live spontaneously—we can avoid the mental traps of grasping for what we want and rejecting what we don't

禪

want. In fact, all such mundane categories will fall away, and we will discover that the ordinary and the holy are identical.

Though this way of thinking may sound very easy, it is the hardest thing in the world to do. We have many fears and expectations that prevent us from acting spontaneously. However, it is worth attempting to act occasionally without deliberation. For example, sometimes the opportunity arises for us to be especially kind, generous, or creative. Often, a feeling of embarrassment or a self-serving excuse arises in our minds that blocks any spontaneous action. Though it may seem to be a contradiction to "plan to be spontaneous," we might find it easier to act in this way if we allow ourselves to become aware of the ways we sabotage the urge. For instance, we may suppress the impulse because we are afraid we will look ridiculous or that our actions will be misunderstood. The truth is, we often fail to act because of our powerful desire to remain in control of the situation.

The next time the opportunity arises for you to do something uncharacteristic but wonderful, remind yourself that the impulse is arising from your ordinary mind, the mind that is identical to your Buddha-nature. Such spontaneous actions may be the shout or blow we need to shock us out of our set ways and give us a glimpse of the freedom of Enlightenment.

禅

Baizhang Huaihai *(720-814)*

Cling to nothing;
crave for nothing.

Mazu had several outstanding disciples. Among them, Baizhang Huaihai is worthy of special attention. Baizhang was born in a remote rural region—in this case, in Fuzhou to the far north, near the Korean border. Well-educated and recognized as a brilliant young man, Baizhang became a monk at Mount Heng, where Mazu had also studied, under the guidance of a well-known Vinaya specialist, Fachao. It was perhaps this early training in the Buddhist monastic code of discipline that spurred Baizhang to develop a new set of rules specifically for use in Zen monasteries. But this work lay in the future.

It is possible that while he was staying at Mount Heng, Baizhang met the aged Nanyue Huairang, the illustrious teacher of Mazu, and was encouraged by him to seek out Mazu for further training. From the start, Baizhang seems to have been one of Mazu's most favored students, for a number of stories tell of their interactions. One such early encounter is said to have resulted in Baizhang's first glimpse of awakening.

It happened this way. After Baizhang had settled in at Mazu's monastery at Zhongling, he approached Mazu for an interview, as was traditional for new arrivals. Instead of speaking, Mazu sat before his pupil in complete silence, staring at a feather duster hanging in a corner of his room.

"If we want to use it, we have to take it from its place," remarked Baizhang.

"If we take your skin from its place, what would become of you?" Mazu retorted.

Baizhang then took the feather duster and held it up.

Mazu then repeated Baizhang's words, "If we want to use it, we have to take it from its place."

Without speaking, Baizhang returned the duster to the place where it had been hanging.

Immediately, Mazu let out a shout so loud that Baizhang lost his hearing for three days.

Later when a concerned fellow monk asked him about his deafness, Baizhang replied, "Deafness? What deafness? After awakening, I just took a rest."

This exchange is typical of the many enigmatic encounters between masters and disciples that have been preserved in the Zen tradition. We are fortunate that these encounters have been annotated by later generations of masters and students. Their comments can help us figure out this curious interaction.

So what was going on between Mazu and Baizhang? First, Baizhang knew that Mazu was testing him during the interview by silently staring at the feather duster. In response, Baizhang made a remark that indicated his understanding of the Zen view of reality. All phenomena of this world, Baizhang was saying, including feather dusters, come from the same "place"—the undifferentiated "suchness" that is the ultimate nature of everything. However, in order for things to be perceived

and used, they must manifest in the world in a multitude of conventional forms, including feather dusters. He then wanted to check if Baizhang understood that the ultimate "suchness" of phenomena and their conventional manifestations always occur as a unity that cannot be separated. His question about Baizhang's skin added a further complexity. Does this unity of ultimate and conventional aspects apply both to objects like the duster and persons like Baizhang himself? By taking up the duster, Baizhang showed that he understood this unity and acknowledged that it applied both to the duster and to him. When Mazu repeated Baizhang's comment, Baizhang returned the duster to its original place, neatly demonstrating that he also realized that the two levels of reality are also identical. Any apparent differences are due to the workings of the deluded mind.

As brilliant as Baizhang's performance had been, Mazu was still not satisfied. As a final comment, he gave out a deafening yell. This shocking sound conveyed an important message. In the course of their encounter, Baizhang interacted with Mazu by speaking to him, which showed Mazu that Baizhang was still responding to reality on a conceptual level. The deafening shout was Mazu's way of demonstrating to Baizhang that he should not rely on words but cut through directly to the Buddha-mind that lies beyond words and thoughts. The shock seems to have done the trick, as Baizhang reported having experienced "awakening" as a result, despite some personal discomfort.

Baizhang spent many years with Mazu, during which time he was no doubt given ample opportunity to further deepen his understanding. Eventually he left to become the abbot of a temple on nearby Mount Daixiong. Apart from the many students he helped, he is particularly known for his efforts to organize Zen monasteries on rigorous principles of morality and self-sufficiency.

禅

TEACHINGS *A New Code of Rules*

By the time Buddhism spread into China during the first century CE, it had existed in India for more than four hundred years. During that time, the Buddha's followers had grown from a few hundred wandering mendicants to a vast organization, with hundreds of large temples and monasteries dotted across the Indian landscape, inhabited by thousands of monks. During his lifetime, the Buddha had laid down some 250 rules to govern the lives of his monastic followers. In subsequent years, a complex code of detailed regulations evolved to keep the communal life of monks proceeding smoothly. This code of morality and behavior, known as the Vinaya, which runs to many hundreds of pages in Sanskrit, was translated into Chinese as part of the Buddhist heritage imported from India.

Buddhist monks in China tried to organize themselves along the lines described in the Indian Vinaya, but they encountered a range of difficulties. Indian culture and customs were so different that it was hard to transpose parts of the Vinaya into a Chinese setting. Sometimes the Vinaya referred to things that did not even exist in China, such as particular kinds of food. Harsh winter weather in northern China also made it difficult for monks to observe Indian rules about diet more suited to a tropical climate.

As we have seen, Baizhang began his career in Zen with a period of intense study of the Vinaya. Thus he would have been familiar with the problems of implementing it faithfully in China. When he became the abbot of his own monastery, Baizhang revised the Vinaya to create a new set of rules for use in his monastery that was more in tune with Chinese requirements.

禪

Though he did not abandon the essence of the Indian monastic code, he did introduce a number of revolutionary changes.

The most noteworthy change was the requirement that monks work to support themselves. Previously, monasteries had depended upon patronage by the nobility, by rich merchants, or even by the imperial household. Though such gifts provided material security, they also tended to tie a monastery to the whims of its patron. Baizhang freed his monks from outside interference by insisting that monasteries become self-sufficient through farming and the manufacture of daily necessities. This new rule, known as the Pure Rule of Baizhang, has not survived in its original form, but Baizhang's reforms were incorporated in a more comprehensive version of the Chinese monastic code that was compiled four hundred years later, during the Yuan Dynasty.

Baizhang's innovations seem to have had even more far-reaching implications. The basic layout of monasteries also changed dramatically around this time. In Zen monasteries, a special hall was constructed to be used by the monks for most of their daily activities. Raised platforms around the walls of this hall provided space for the monks to sleep, eat, and do their meditation practice, though communal worship and other ceremonies were still held in a separate Buddha hall.

As a result of Baizhang's developments, the monks also worked in the fields and workshops attached to the monastery. This arrangement was so successful that the his new rule and financial plan for monastic organization was eventually adopted throughout China, even by Buddhist schools not affiliated with the Zen tradition.

禪

LESSON *Combining Work with Meditation*

Since many Buddhist practitioners today do not live in monasteries, Baizhang's innovations to the Vinaya may not seem very relevant. But the inspiration that inspired these changes, the combination of work with meditation, contains a valuable lesson for all of us.

Baizhang's idea can be summed up in his famous slogan: "A day of no work is a day of no food." Baizhang was quite insistent on this rule and did not make exceptions to it even for himself in his old age. When he was weak and in failing health, he still worked daily in the vegetable garden. Taking pity on their revered master, some of his monks hid his gardening tools. But Baizhang refused to eat that day, since he had not worked! The monks had no choice but to return the tools in order to restore harmony to the monastery.

Most of us do not have generous patrons but need to work for our living. Thus we might consider ourselves to be self-sufficient. Though our daily work may not literally be the reason we eat each day, if we did not work, we could not support ourselves with the necessities of life. However, this kind of self-sufficiency is only the superficial level of Baizhang's message. Many of us work simply to earn money. We can't wait for work to end each day, or for weekends and vacations to arrive, so that work can end and our "real life" can begin. Baizhang's rule was intended to overcome this split between activity and leisure,

work and meditation. He understood that combining work with spiritual practice could transform any tedious chore into a path toward spiritual development.

There are several ways to transform your daily experience of work into spiritual practice. First, consider your occupation. For a Buddhist, it is preferable that your job do nothing to exploit or harm other beings. For example, working as a medical researcher who tests drugs on laboratory animals is unwholesome from a spiritual point of view. Other jobs today might involve varying levels of deceit and dishonesty, such as writing for a tabloid newspaper that harms the reputations of famous people. Basically, if your job harms beings or creates an atmosphere of greed, competition, and exploitation, maybe it is time for a change.

If your job is acceptable in spiritual terms, the next step is to try to integrate some aspects of meditation into your day. Ask yourself, are you "present in the moment" when you are working, or is your mind somewhere else? Try to train yourself to focus on the here and now and to be mindful of what you are doing, without letting your thoughts wander off. The technique is quite similar to more formal meditation. Just as you might concentrate on your breathing to the exclusion of everything else, so too when you work, focus your attention on whatever task you are engaged in. When your mind wanders off, note that your attention has drifted and refocus it on the matter at hand.

禪

At a still deeper level, Baizhang is also asking us to reevaluate our attitude toward working. On one occasion, he said, "Cling to nothing; crave for nothing." If you are engaged in a high-stress job just for the sake of earning a large salary, ask yourself whether you have made the best choice. We all need a basic level of income to support ourselves and our families, but do we really need extra money to buy gadgets and luxury items? Do these things really make us happy? Could it be that we cling to our possessions and yearn for still more as a way of blocking out a void in the soul that things can never fill?

Baizhang would tell you that you will be happier if you simplify your needs and learn to be content with what you have. Consuming less leaves more resources for others, including people in other parts of the world. Baizhang would say that you are only truly self-sufficient when you do not deprive others of what they need, even indirectly.

禪

Zhaozhou Congshen *(778-897)*

"What is the way?"
"The ordinary mind is the way."

Well known from the many recorded stories and dialogues in which he is involved, Zhaozhou was one of the most remarkable Zen Masters of the late Tang period. Despite this fame, he is an enigmatic figure, for few facts are known about his life. He was born in a small town in northern China in present-day Shandong Province. As a young man, he became a monk at the famous Shaolin Monastery on Mount Song and completed the basic monastic training. He then sought out the great Nanquan Puyuan (748-835), a disciple of Mazu Daoyi, for further guidance.

Soon after his arrival at Nanquan's monastery, Zhaozhou went to see Nanquan for instruction.

"What is the way?" asked Zhaozhou, getting straight to the point.

"The ordinary mind is the way," replied Nanquan.

Zhaozhou then asked a beginner's question, "May I direct myself toward it or not?"

"To seek is to deviate," answered Nanquan in true Zen style.

Perplexed, Zhaozhou then asked Nanquan, "If I do not seek it, how can I know about it?"

Nanquan summed up the Zen approach succinctly in his reply. "The way is unconnected with knowing and not knowing. Knowing is to have a concept, while not knowing is to be ignorant. If you realize the way that is beyond doubt, it is like the sky—vast open emptiness. How can one affirm or deny it?"

Hearing this reply, Zhaozhou had his first flash of awakening. It is reported that his mind became clear like the full moon.

Following this exchange, Zhaozhou stayed with Nanquan for thirty years, apparently acting as his devoted deputy and trusted companion. Records of the sayings of the Zen Masters tell many stories of the delightful though often enigmatic interactions between these two gifted men. One famous story tells of the two arguing over a cat.

One day, while Zhaozhou was away from the monastery, Nanquan faced the assembled monks. Holding up a cat, he said, "Say something appropriate, and the cat will be spared. If you don't, I'll kill it!"

The monks stared in silence, unable to speak, so Nanquan cut the poor cat in two.

When evening fell, Zhaozhou returned to the monastery. Nanquan told him what had happened. Zhaozhou then removed his sandals, placed them on his head, and went out.

At this, Nanquan said, "If you had been there, the cat would have been saved!"

Students of Zen have argued long about the significance of this story. It seems clear that from Nanquan's point of view, the whole interchange is not really about a cat. Nanquan wanted the assembled monks to say something to convince him that even one of them had an authentic view of reality. By their silence, they demonstrated their ignorance. Since none of the monks

禪

could rise to the challenge, Nanquan cut the cat in half—hard luck for the cat but a dramatic teaching for the deluded monks. The cutting knife would have been an obvious symbol of the incisive insight of a Buddha, which is sometimes represented by a razor sharp sword that cuts through all delusions. When Zhaozhou returned, he took off his traveling sandals to demonstrate that he had returned home on a conventional level, while on a higher level, he had completed his spiritual journey by eliminating attachment. Zhaozhou's clever mime would have answered Nanquan's challenge and saved the cat.

When Zhaozhou was fifty-seven years old, Nanquan died. After a three-year period of mourning, Zhaozhou packed his bags and embarked on a life of wandering, which he continued for the next twenty years. During this long interval, we can see Zhaozhou's preference for humble anonymity. In many ways,

this course of action was wise and even necessary, for the years immediately following Nanquan's death were marked by anti-Buddhist persecutions ordered by the mad emperor, Wuzong.

Influenced by the Daoist hostility toward Buddhism, Wuzong took steps to restrict it. A period of destruction ensued, during which many monasteries and temples were closed down and their occupants forced to return to lay life. Fortunately for Buddhism in China, Wuzong died suddenly in 846, just as he was about to promulgate further restrictions against Buddhism.

Under Wuzong's successors, hostility toward Buddhism ended. By this time, Zhaozhou was eighty. Finally ending his travels, he took up residence in a dilapidated temple in Hebei Province near Beijing. There he lived modestly for another forty years until his death, teaching the few disciples who could endure the harsh conditions found in the remote northern provinces.

禪

TEACHINGS *Inventiveness and Humor*

Zhaozhou apparently left no writings of his own, but we do have records of his encounters and dialogues with other masters and with monks under his care. If Mazu and Deshan used blows and shouts to teach others (see Chapters 6 and 9), one might say that Zhaozhou relied on inventiveness and humor. Many of his deeds were very strange and defy easy explanation, and his utterances were often paradoxical or incongruous. But in his exchanges with other monks, we catch glimpses of the exuberant playfulness that arises from high spiritual attainment.

For example, during his time at Nanquan's monastery, Zhaozhou was once in charge of tending the fires at the monastery. One day while everybody was out working in the garden, Zhaozhou went into the monks' hall and shouted, "Help, fire! Help, fire!" Of course, everybody rushed back to the hall in a panic. They found no fire, only Zhaozhou shouting from inside the hall, with the door shut firmly behind him. The monks were at a loss what to do. Finally, Nanquan took the key from its hook outside the door and threw it into the hall through the window, despite the fact that the keyhole for the lock on the door was on the outside.

Did Zhaozhou carry out this prank to amuse himself or did he have a more profound motive? It seems probable that he and Nanquan devised this incident as a way of testing the monks. For you see, the fire that Zhaozhou was shouting about was not the conflagration that the monks feared but the inner fires of passion and delusion. Understanding this, Nanquan threw the key inside where it would be useless to Zhaozhou had there been a real fire. By this action, Nanquan was demonstrating that we are each responsible for our own predicament, from which only we can extricate ourselves. A master can point the way, but the student has to do the work—something that we often forget when we encounter our own teachers.

Zhaozhou's iconoclastic humor shines forth in his dialogues, such as the following instance:

A monk asked him, "What is that which is spiritual?"

Zhaozhou said, "A puddle of piss in the Pure Land."

The monk said, "I ask you to reveal it to me."

Zhaozhou said, "Don't tempt me."

By this Zhaozhou tried to convey that the spiritual can be found in everyday life. There is no contradiction between pure and impure. Both are merely labels, and all categories are a matter of perspective.

In a similar vein, we read another amusing story:

Once while Zhaozhou was in the toilet, he called out to Wenyuan.

Wenyuan answered, "Yes?"

Zhaozhou said, "I'm in the toilet now and needn't expound the Dharma any further for you."

In other words, going to the toilet is an expression of the

禪

Dharma, as are all natural, everyday activities. In essence, Zhaozhou was saying, if the true Dharma can be found even in the toilet, where can it not be found? Zen Masters like Zhaozhou liked to stress that because Buddha-nature is always present, awakening and insight can come about even through the most humble daily activities. This understanding can often be a great source of comfort and encouragement when we find ourselves in less than ideal situations.

禅

LESSON *Spiritual Jokes and Pranks*

How do you expect enlightened people to behave? We all tend to hold an image of the archetypal religious teacher: The teacher should be wise, calm, austere, and grave, taking everything seriously with an air of quiet inner peace. Buddhist teachers do act this way on some occasions, but we fail to do justice to them, or to the state of Enlightenment, if we expect our teachers to act that way all the time. When we hear the words of great Buddhist masters of the past, we often forget that they were just like us in many ways and enjoyed a laugh and a joke. However, the humor of such teachers usually had a deeper purpose. A careful read of the dialogues of the Buddha shows that even he had a good sense of humor and would use it to guide his listeners to a more profound level of understanding.

As we have seen, Zen Masters like Zhaozhou positively reveled in jokes and pranks. We have already looked at one example of Zhaozhou's practical jokes, his calling out "Fire!" when no real fire existed. The records of his sayings and deeds are full of similar stories, even if the humor of his tricks was not immediately apparent to those on the receiving end. Zhaozhou seemed to use incongruous humor as a way of jolting people out of their spiritual ruts. The technique had the same purpose and seemed to be as effective as a sudden shout or the whack of a master's stick.

When Zhaozhou first arrived at Nanquan's monastery, he could not resist a little humor, even at his first meeting with Nanquan. Entering Nanquan's room, Zhaozhou found Nanquan lying down. Nanquan asked Zhaozhou where he had come from, to which Zhaozhou replied, "I've come from Ruixiang." Now Nanquan knew, though most of us don't, that Ruixang, which literally means "omen figure," is the site of a large Buddha statue. Nanquan next asked Zhaozhou if he had seen the famous standing Buddha. Cleverly combining respect with humor, Zhaozhou answered, "No, but I've seen a reclining Buddha," alluding to Nanquan lying down before him.

This story gives us a glimpse into the way in which Zen masters loved to play with words. It is often difficult for us, living over a thousand years later in a culture with different assumptions and values, to appreciate the subtle messages of these interchanges when we read about them. Though the spiritual message may come through, we often miss half the fun because we don't understand the word play and the frequent use of puns. In a similar vein, we have seen that many Zen Masters hit their

禅

students with their canes and sometimes got hit back. But perhaps we take these accounts too literally. It is possible that these episodes of apparent violence were nothing of the sort. They may actually have been bouts of slapstick clowning between consenting parties who all enjoyed the joke.

Enlightenment is a serious business, but being serious all the time is not a sign of Enlightenment. Classical descriptions of the attributes of Enlightenment mention that it is characterized by great bliss and joy. This joy is precisely what we see in so many stories that are told about the great Zen Masters: the overflowing enthusiasm of awakening often manifested in crazy behavior and outrageous jokes. Indeed, beware a teacher who does not laugh and joke! A teacher who lacks a sense of humor may be taking himself or herself too seriously. An absence of joy and enthusiasm may indicate that a spiritual teacher still has far to travel on the path toward realization.

Compare your teacher's sense of humor with that of Zhaozhou as revealed in the following dialogue:

An official once asked Zhaozhou, "Will you go to hell or not?"

Zhaozhou replied, "I entered hell a long time ago."

"So, why did you enter hell?" the worried official asked.

Back came Zhaozhou's reply, "If I don't enter hell, who will teach you?"

So, when you next read an anthology of Zen sayings and deeds, remember that half the stories are jokes. Most do have a serious point, but they are also intended to make you laugh. If you resist the notion that religious instruction can be humorous, maybe it's time to ask yourself whether you are taking yourself and your spiritual quest too seriously. Do you attend centers for meditation and instruction feeling heavy and gloomy, almost as if you were attending a funeral? If so, remind yourself that laughter can release pent up or blocked emotions that hinder your spiritual growth. Moreover, laughter helps you to appreciate the incongruity and ridiculousness of many of your everyday assumptions.

I remember one occasion when I was leading a small group in reciting mantras. When we came to a particular mantra, first one person and then another began to chuckle. After a while everybody was doubled up with laughter. There was no disrespect in this. I like to think that our laughter was actually a sign that the mantra had manifested some of its power. Though unseen by us, I'll bet the Buddha was watching and joining in with the laughter, full of joy at our small measure of progress.

Deshan Xuanjian *(782-865)*

*All the profound doctrines are but a speck of dust
in a vast void.
All the great affairs of the world are but a drop
of water cast into a bottomless chasm.*

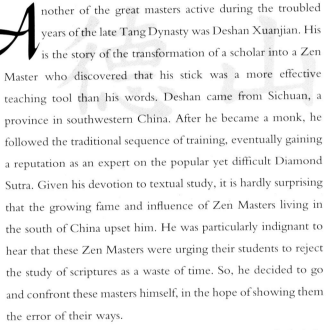

Another of the great masters active during the troubled years of the late Tang Dynasty was Deshan Xuanjian. His is the story of the transformation of a scholar into a Zen Master who discovered that his stick was a more effective teaching tool than his words. Deshan came from Sichuan, a province in southwestern China. After he became a monk, he followed the traditional sequence of training, eventually gaining a reputation as an expert on the popular yet difficult Diamond Sutra. Given his devotion to textual study, it is hardly surprising that the growing fame and influence of Zen Masters living in the south of China upset him. He was particularly indignant to hear that these Zen Masters were urging their students to reject the study of scriptures as a waste of time. So, he decided to go and confront these masters himself, in the hope of showing them the error of their ways.

While traveling to the south, armed with copies of scholarly commentaries on the Diamond Sutra, he happened to stop at the stall of an old woman selling snacks by the roadside. As she served him, she asked Deshan what he was carrying in his bundle. When he told her that he was carrying commentaries on the Diamond Sutra, she said that she had a question for him. If he could answer it to her satisfaction, she would let him have the food for free.

The old woman then asked the following question: "In the Diamond Sutra it says, 'The past mind cannot be attained; the present mind cannot be attained; and the future mind cannot be attained.' What I want to know is, which mind are you refreshing right now?" To appreciate this question, we must understand that the idiomatic Chinese phrase for snack means literally "refreshing the mind."

Deshan was speechless, since his scholarly training had not prepared him to answer this type of question. He soon realized that this kind of inquiry was what lay in store for him when he confronted the masters of the south. Seeing Deshan's discomfort, the old woman suggested that he go to see a master by the name of Longtan Chongxin.

Taking the old woman's advice, Deshan traveled to Longtan's monastery. Soon after arriving there, he went to see the master for an interview. It was evening and the sun had gone down. When Deshan entered the master's room, Longtan said, "It's getting late, so you should go now."

Perhaps a little puzzled, Deshan bade Longtan good night and started to go out of the room, remarking, "It's dark outside."

Longtan then lit a candle and held it out to Deshan. But just as Deshan reached for it, Longtan blew the candle out.

The significance of this brief encounter hit Deshan like a thunderbolt. Immediately, he experienced a burst of awakening. In the light of this experience, Deshan saw, as many before and after him have done, that his treasured books were insignificant as compared to the direct experience of realization.

Students of Zen have interpreted the encounter this way: When Deshan commented that it was dark outside, Longtan decided to use the remark as a teaching opportunity. By lighting a candle and holding it out to Deshan, he signaled that the darkness can be seen as a metaphor for Deshan's ignorance. By reaching for the candle, Deshan showed that he was aware of the darkness of ignorance and that he accepted that Longtan could teach him the way to enlighten this darkness. But by blowing the candle out, Longtan gave the further message that Deshan must not rely on exterior solutions, for only generating an inner light could enlighten his darkness.

The very next day Deshan burned his commentaries on the Diamond Sutra in front of the Dharma Hall, commenting that,

"All the profound doctrines are but a speck of dust in a vast void. All the great affairs of the world are but a drop of water cast into a bottomless chasm."

After spending some time deepening his understanding of the Zen approach, Deshan became an established master in his own right. As a scholar, he had relied on words. As a master, he became known for using his staff. Deshan had discovered that it is too easy for a student to come up with a clever but superficial answer to a question. A whack of the stick on a student's back, however, served to push the student beyond the confines of dualistic thinking. Even the threat of a whack seemed to do the trick. One of Deshan's favorite ploys was to wave his staff in the air, shouting "Thirty blows if you can speak; thirty blows if you can't speak!"

禅

TEACHINGS *No Armchair Buddhism*

Though Deshan ultimately rejected the Diamond Sutra in favor of direct experience, this text was actually very influential as a source of inspiration among masters of the Southern School of Zen. The Diamond Sutra is part of large collection of Mahayana scriptures known as the Perfection of Insight Sutras. These texts deal with the difficult concept of "emptiness," the Buddha's teachings concerning the nonexistence of a permanent and independent self.

As a means to establish the nonexistence of the ego-self, the Buddha taught several systems for breaking down a person into component elements. For example, he said that each individual is composed of five psychophysical components: matter, feeling, ideation, motivation, and consciousness. Through meditation, it can be established that none of these elements is identical to the ego-self, as each is impermanent. For instance, the meditator asks: Am I my body? Am I my feelings? Am I my thoughts? Am I my emotions? In each case, investigation proves that the self is not identical to any of these components. The goal of such contemplation is the realization that the self does not exist in the way we typically perceive it.

The same analytical process, breaking down wholes into parts, can be applied to the world at large. Meditative investigation shows that any element of the world outside ourselves, such as a table or a tree, can be similarly deconstructed into component

parts. Thus a tree is neither its leaves, nor its roots, nor its branches. The concept of "tree" is merely a convenient label that we apply to a constellation of component elements that lacks any true and substantial reality. In fact, all things and persons are an impermanent constellation of components that exist only as a result of a train of causes and effects. Thus the components of a tree exist only as a temporary result of the causes of a seed, the fertile earth, the sun, and rainwater. This total lack of any abiding reality to persons and objects is what is meant by "emptiness."

Deshan and other Zen Masters did not downplay the importance of Buddhist scriptures because they disrespected them or thought that study was a waste of time. Rather they knew that people would tend to become too involved in the intellectual concepts described in the scriptures, rather like armchair philosophers. Just because you can understand the meaning of a sentence, define the words, and relate one passage of scripture to another does not mean that you have moved any closer to Enlightenment. Skill in reading and interpreting texts can be very misleading, because knowledge of the text can be mistaken for experiential understanding. A reliance on texts is rather like a person who spends years studying and writing about wine by examining the labels, studying the shape of the bottles, and reading what other people have said, without ever having tasted the wine for himself.

To show their contempt for such "armchair Buddhists," Deshan and other masters sometimes used shocking language to insult the elements of Buddhism held dear by scholars and simple-minded pious followers. The following is quite typical of Deshan writing in this vein:

I don't hold to some views about the patriarchs. Here there are no patriarchs and no Buddhas. Bodhidharma is a stinking old foreigner. Shakyamuni is a dried piece of shit. Manjushri and Samantabhadra are dung carriers. The so-called "realizing the mystery" is nothing but breaking through to grab an ordinary person's life. Enlightenment and Nirvana are a donkey's tethering post. The twelve classes of scripture are devils' texts, just paper for wiping infected boils. The four fruitions, the original mind, and the ten stages are just ghosts guarding a graveyard. They will never save you.

Strong stuff! But if, as Deshan maintained, Enlightenment must be experienced directly, then no amount of reading and pious practice will help you release your Buddha-nature from the veil of obscurations. Study without practice will just blow out the candle of illumination you seek. Study certainly has its place in all forms of Buddhism but there is always the danger that it can become a seductive substitute for the real hard work involved when the teachings are put into practice. Yet, for us in the West an initial familiarity with the basic teachings of Buddhism is essential if our practice is to succeed.

禅

LESSON *Getting Down to Basics*

So, if you must not pin your hopes for awakening upon reading and studying Buddhist scriptures, what are you to do?

First, note that Zen Masters like Deshan who came to denounce the study of texts were themselves very familiar with the concepts and ideas of the Buddhist scriptures. Reading about Buddhism and gaining a sound familiarity with basic concepts is a very desirable place to begin. But Deshan would have you remember that study is only a means to an end. Of course, it is perfectly possible to engage in Zen meditation practice without knowing much about the concepts of Buddhism, providing that you have access to a good teacher who can guide you through the process. However, for most of us, some knowledge of terms and ideas is very useful. The caution we can take from Deshan is to beware of becoming too obsessed with concepts and getting sidetracked into useless speculation. The Buddha himself viewed his teachings as merely a means to an end, to be abandoned when they had served their purpose.

Deshan counseled that seekers should get down to basics. On one occasion he said:

When there is nothing more within you, do not engage in useless seeking. What is found by useless seeking is no gain. When your mind is without anything and you are no-mind, then you are free and spiritual, empty and marvelous.

When Deshan said that "there is nothing more within," he meant that beneath all concepts and all speculations, Buddha-nature lies within you. It does not need to be developed or improved in any way. Once you can accept that this potential for Enlightenment lies within you, avoid getting hung up on explaining or rationalizing it. Simply accept that Buddha-nature is there, and that's that! To speculate about it further, to think that you have to do something special to become enlightened, is what Deshan meant by "useless seeking." Any complicated knowledge about Buddhahood that you acquire in this way is a waste of time.

Enlightenment is a process of emptying rather than one of filling and acquiring. Following the teachings of other Zen Masters such as Baizhang, put effort instead into simplifying your life and eliminating as many attachments as possible. Aim to be as spontaneous as Mazu and Zhaozhou, putting aside all prejudgments and goal-orientated actions. By getting down to basics—the basic realization of your own intrinsic Buddha-nature—you become, as Deshan put it, free and spiritual, empty and marvelous.

禪

禅

Linji Yixuan *(810?-866)*

When hunger comes, I eat my rice;
When sleep comes, I close my eyes.
Fools laugh at me,
but the wise understand.

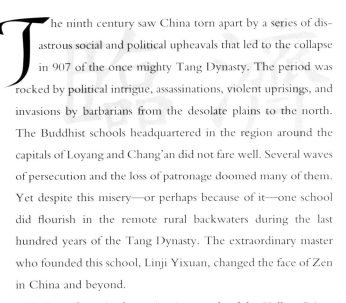

The ninth century saw China torn apart by a series of disastrous social and political upheavals that led to the collapse in 907 of the once mighty Tang Dynasty. The period was rocked by political intrigue, assassinations, violent uprisings, and invasions by barbarians from the desolate plains to the north. The Buddhist schools headquartered in the region around the capitals of Loyang and Chang'an did not fare well. Several waves of persecution and the loss of patronage doomed many of them. Yet despite this misery—or perhaps because of it—one school did flourish in the remote rural backwaters during the last hundred years of the Tang Dynasty. The extraordinary master who founded this school, Linji Yixuan, changed the face of Zen in China and beyond.

Linji was born in the region just south of the Yellow River in present-day Shandong Province. His biographies tell us that he was a gifted child whose abilities soon became apparent to those around him. In his lectures, Linji mentions a few details of his studies after becoming a monk. Like most Zen Masters, he gained a thorough grounding in traditional Buddhist doctrines and practices, including the Vinaya and Buddhist scriptures. But Linji soon became dissatisfied with this conventional training. Leaving the monastery where he had been living, he made his way south to seek a more vigorous path to Enlightenment.

He was still a young man, about twenty-six, when he arrived at the monastery of the Zen Master Huangbo (?–850) at Hongzhou. Though some Zen Masters achieved a taste of awakening soon after establishing contact with a suitable teacher, for Linji the path to realization was not easy. Apparently, Linji lived at Huangbo's monastery for some three years without making progress. He seems to have kept his distance from Huangbo as though something did not quite click between master and student. Perhaps aware of Linji's difficulty, Huangbo suggested that Linji visit another master, Dayu, a former student of Mazu, who was living in a hermitage in the same region. What happened next makes us suspect that Huangbo and Dayu were in collusion behind Linji's back, with Huangbo playing the role of the nice guy and Dayu the nasty one.

禪

Taking Huangbo's advice, Linji traveled to Dayu's hermitage. When the two sat down to talk, Linji tried to impress Dayu with his deep knowledge of the Buddhist scriptures, generally a bad move when dealing with a Zen Master. Dayu responded to this show of erudition by giving poor Linji a sound beating with his cane. Returning to Huangbo, Linji described this painful encounter. However, Huangbo encouraged Linji kindly to go back to Dayu and persevere.

So, once again Linji made his way to see Dayu, who greeted him gruffly. "So you're not ashamed of yourself? Why have you come back?" Dayu shouted while reaching for his cane.

Again Linji got a beating, but this time something extraordinary happened. One particularly sharp blow triggered an awakening in Linji, though Dayu failed to notice this. Thrown out the next morning, Linji went back to Huangbo and joyfully told him about his awakening experience. We can only speculate why this rather painful encounter with Dayu led to Linji's awakening, but clearly the spiritual work that Linji had been doing had prepared him for a breakthrough. He tells us in his later writings that he gained realization only through "exhaustive investigation and grinding discipline." We might say that in returning to Dayu for a second beating, Linji demonstrated the proper attitude of grim determination tinged with desperation, rather like the Buddha himself who vowed to remain sitting under the Bodhi tree until either death or Enlightenment. If only we too had that degree of courage to motivate our efforts!

禪

As etiquette demanded, Linji went back to see Dayu a week later. Ever ready with his cane, Dayu was just about to beat Linji again for his impudence in returning, when Linji turned the tables. He grabbed the cane from Dayu's hand and began beating Dayu instead. At that instant, Dayu realized with delight that Linji had awakened. It is interesting that Dayu did not take credit for bringing about this change in Linji but said later that it was Huangbo who had set things in motion.

Linji lived in this area for another decade, dividing his time between Huangbo and Dayu. Soon after Dayu's death, around 850, Linji took his leave from Huangbo and embarked on a period of wandering. Eventually Linji settled at a monastery by a river near the mountain pilgrimage site of Wutaishan. Because of its location, this monastery was called *Linji-yuan*, the "monastery by the ford." It is from this place that Linji took his popular name.

Hidden away in the mountains with harsh winters and few luxuries, Linji did not gather a huge following like some of his contemporaries. In fact, he had only a handful of students whose numbers were increased from time to time by pilgrims on their way to the sacred mountain of Wutaishan. Yet he must have gained a considerable reputation as a teacher because he was visited by several renowned masters, such as Zhaozhou, as well as winning the admiration and respect of the local governor.

Beyond the few hints in the collected record of his sayings, little is known about Linji's later life. Like a flame that burns brightest before it is extinguished, Linji died in his early fifties.

禪

TEACHINGS *The Sayings of Linji*

Linji's spiritual legacy was enormous, for although he was not blessed with great numbers of disciples, he achieved fame through his spiritual descendants. By the beginning of the Song Dynasty (960–1279), the Linji school had become the predominant form of Zen in China. Beyond China, the Linji school was influential in Korea, Vietnam and, above all, Japan, where it has survived to the present day as the Rinzai school. Over the centuries, Linji's devoted followers virtually deified him, glorifying his memory with effusive praise, such as the following tribute from the thirteenth-century introduction to the Collected Sayings of Linji: "He is like a snow-white elephant king, like a golden-haired lion; when he crouches to jump and roars, the hearts and brains of jackals and wild foxes burst . . . heaven turns and earth revolves as Linji moves freely in all directions."

Many sayings and sermons attributed to the early Zen Masters have survived, but these often come down to us through the hands of devout students who polished the words of the master and sometimes added material from a later date to bolster the master's reputation. Though it, too, was probably edited and expanded in this way, the Collected Sayings of Linji (*Linji yü-lu*) is one of the first such books through which we can still hear the authentic voice of the master. Linji's followers apparently recorded verbatim many of his sayings and discourses, which were published in one volume about 150 years after his death.

The appeal of Linji's sayings had much to do with the state of Zen at the time when they were published. Many Zen Masters of the Tang period when Linji lived warned their disciples of the dangers of relying exclusively on the written word, but like Linji, they had studied the Buddhist scriptures before beginning Zen practice. However, by the Song period when Linji's sayings were published, many Zen practitioners had decided that it was too much bother to study the scriptures at all. They found ample justification for this view in Linji's Sayings. Linji denigrated study of and commentary on the Buddhist scriptures in very harsh terms: "They seize upon ideas from the scriptures to discuss and compose commentaries. This is like putting a lump of shit in your mouth, then spitting it out for others to eat." Linji was suspicious of the use of language in general. He warned his students that speech about the Dharma can never be helpful or true: "As soon as you open your mouths, it already has nothing to do with it," he wrote, for "verbal explanations have no basis."

These misgivings about language may account for Linji's rough behavior, which combined the worst of the beatings and shouts used by Mazu and Dayu. At times, Linji's actions seem almost pathological. Again and again we read: "Linji saw a monk coming. The monk bowed, and Linji hit him." End of the story. Nor did Linji feel any qualms about hitting women. One story tells of his visit to the master Fengling. On the way, Linji asked an old woman if Fengling was at home.

禅

"At the moment Fengling is not there," the old woman replied.

When Linji asked her if she knew where Fengling had gone, the old woman walked off.

So, Linji called her back and punched her!

Linji explained this seemingly incomprehensible behavior this way: "Most who study the Path try to depend on things to do, so I start hitting them from there. If they use their hands, I hit them on the hands; if they use their mouths, I hit them in the mouth; if they use their eyes, I hit them in the eyes."

Nor did Linji support meditation as an appropriate Dharma practice. In his youth when he was studying under Huangbo, Linji seems not to have been very rigorous in his own meditation practice. Another monk saw him sleeping on the cushion and reported this fact to Huangbo. Rather than punishing Linji, Huangbo praised him, saying "There's somebody meditating properly." Later, when he became a teacher himself, Linji criticized meditation as a waste of time: "Even if you gain something from meditative practice, it is just the karma of birth and death . . . If you fixate your mind and contemplate stillness, hold up your mind for outer awareness and hold in your mind for inner realization, freeze your mind and enter stable concentration, this is all contrived activity. . . . You sit leaning against a wall with your tongue pressed to the roof of your mouth, motionless in profound clarity. You think this is the way of the patriarchs. How wrong you are!"

禅

Given all of this, it's not surprising that Linji also had no time for conventional Buddhist practices aimed at developing virtue, as he wrote: "They say that Enlightenment can be attained . . . when you guard yourself from the misdeeds of body, speech, and mind, but this kind of talk is like the springtime showers."

So, just what did Linji teach his followers? The overall impression a modern reader gets of Linji's monastery is that it was very much like a rather strict boot camp. Like a tough drill sergeant, Linji greeted new recruits by cutting them down to size: "You run around as a shallow adherent with your bowl, sack, and shitty burdens seeking the Dharma." As time went by, beginners would learn that Linji demanded that they totally abandon all striving for truth, all attachments, and all "religious" activities. Thus he instructed his disciples: "The Dharma is effortless. Just be without concerns in your ordinary life, as you shit and piss, wear clothes and eat food; when tired, lie down . . . It is just a matter of passing the time without concerns." Thinking and the use of language apart from simple everyday communications were also forbidden: "Just manage to put a stop to your thoughts and do not do any more external seeking," he said, further warning his disciples, "If you go on this way accepting empty words as real things, you are making a great mistake."

In essence, Linji's training focused on eliminating every facet of human behavior that obscured the innate Buddha-mind of his disciples. His violence, shouts, and irrational sayings were intended to empty the minds of his students of all thoughts and concepts so that their inherent Buddha-mind could shine forth. When Linji did resort to the more conventional approach of formal lectures, his message merely reflected his style of training. All the disciples needed was the faith that they did have Buddha-mind:

Students today can't get anywhere: what's wrong with you all? A lack of faith in yourself, that's what's wrong! If you don't have any faith in yourself, you'll just be in a flurry trying to keep up with things in your bewilderment; you'll be tossed about by whatever situation you find yourself in without ever having any real freedom.

Linji never described concretely how his students were to generate this self-reliant faith, but he implied that the best way was to give up expectations. As he told them, if you have no expectations, you'll never face disappointment. Instead, you'll just flow with events and get on with everyday life. He summarized this approach in one of his most famous sayings:

When hunger comes, I eat my rice;
When sleep comes, I close my eyes.
Fools laugh at me,
but the wise understand.

LESSON *Doing What Comes Naturally*

Though you may not wish to subject yourself to the kind of rigid discipline Linji advocated, there are two aspects of Linji's teachings that you might try to implement. First, Linji advised that you drop all pretensions and aspirations, including the mystery and ritual that surrounds religion. In fact, to be true to Linji, you should drop religion altogether! Linji often claimed that what is truly spiritual is to be found in the ordinariness of everyday life. As Linji said, "The way I see things, there's no need for anything special. Just do what comes naturally . . . pass the time doing nothing."

So to follow Linji's advice, take the rest of the day off from being religious. Instead, try living in the present moment. When you cook food, cook food with your whole attention. When you eat, do not read, or watch television, or converse. Just eat. If you find your mind wandering off, hopping around from distraction to distraction, bring it back to whatever you are doing, and do whatever it is simply and naturally.

The second aspect of Linji's teachings that you may wish to implement is his concern with the misuse of language. Many of us are virtually drowning in words in our daily lives and seem to have an almost pathological fear of silence. Take stock of your own addiction to language. Are you one of those people who turns on the television or radio as soon as they get home? Do you use electronic noise as a kind of background wallpaper to block out loneliness and inconvenient thoughts? How many books, magazines, and newspapers do you look at each day? How much time do you spend talking on the telephone or reading and responding to e-mails?

You can be sure Linji would not have approved of our modern reliance on language. After smashing your TV and your other electronic gadgets, he might have shouted at you to shut up! However, you don't need to break anything to try being silent for a while. Many religions, not only Buddhism, recognize the value of silent retreats. If your life allows, arrange a period of time, perhaps an afternoon, or a twenty-four hour period, or a whole weekend, in which you can practice silence. During this time, do not speak, read, or listen to anything. Engage in your everyday activities with full attention, trying to stay focused on the task at hand. After a while, you may find that the chatter in your head starts to quiet down as well, and that you are learning to appreciate and enjoy the sound of silence.

禪

禅

Yunmen Wenyan *(864-949)*

"It is better if I do not speak and thus deceive you."

From the middle of the eighth century, China entered a period of instability, strife, and invasion. The centralized authority of the Tang Dynasty collapsed and by 907 was replaced by a group of small independent kingdoms known as the Five Dynasties in the north and the Ten Kingdoms in the south. The situation in the north was made even more desperate by a series of devastating famines. Eventually order was restored and the country was reunified in 960 with the establishment of the Song Dynasty in the north with its capital at Kaifeng.

China was a very different place than it had been in the heyday of the Tang rulers. Its political and military influence, which had once extended as far as Iran, was restricted to the heartlands, and a mood of xenophobia pervaded the land. Buddhism as a whole fared badly during this period, with the main schools losing much of their power as their rich patrons perished. The early years of the Song Dynasty did see a brief revival of contact with India, the homeland of the Dharma, and a small group of Indian monks once again made their way to China to transmit and translate new texts. Toward the end of the tenth century, a revolutionary development in the dissemination of Buddhism occurred, the first printing of the entire Buddhist canon of texts from tens of thousands of individually carved woodblocks. This new printing technology had a profound effect on Zen, as it made possible the publication of many records of the discourses and sayings of the Zen Masters of the Tang period.

In this turbulent era, the twilight of Zen's golden age, Yunmen Wenyan, the last truly great Chinese Zen Master, was born in the coastal town of Jiaxing, southwest of present-day Shanghai. His early life followed the pattern with which we are familiar: entry into a monastery, intensive study of the Vinaya and scriptures, and a period of wandering as a spiritual pilgrim. On these travels, Yunmen encountered Muzhou Daoming, a gifted though rather eccentric disciple of Huangbo, the ninth-century master who was one of the main teachers of Linji.

Muzhou was renowned for his fearsome methods of training, and Yunmen experienced these most painfully right from the start. After arriving at Muzhou's monastery, Yunmen went to the master's room, as was customary, to ask for teachings. When Muzhou heard Yunmen's footsteps in the corridor outside, he slammed the door shut. Yunmen knocked, and Muzhou gruffly demanded to know who it was.

Bravely, Yunmen replied, "It's me. I'm not clear about life, and I want you to give me instructions."

Muzhou opened his door, took one look at Yunmen, and slammed it shut again.

The next day, Yunmen tried again, but the same thing happened. Not to be deterred, Yunmen went a third time to Muzhou's door. This time, before Muzhou could shut the door, Yunmen stuck his foot into the doorway.

"Well," shouted Muzhou, "Speak! Speak!"

Yunmen began to stutter a few words, but Muzhou grabbed him and bellowed, "Too late!" With that, Muzhou slammed the heavy door shut with such force that it caught Yunmen's leg and broke it. Gasping in pain, Yunmen attained his first awakening.

One way of understanding this event is to note that Yunmen spoke of "I" when he addressed Muzhou. By refusing him entry, Muzhou was demonstrating that concepts of "I" always result in a closed door, a spiritual barrier. Breaking Yunmen's leg was an effective way for Muzhou to generate a state of non-self in Yunmen. It is, after all, difficult to entertain conceptual thoughts about an "I" and "teachings" when you are in excruciating pain!

After staying with Muzhou for a while, Yunmen was sent to study with Xuefeng Yicun, a disciple of Deshan and one of the most famous masters alive at that time. Like Muzhou, Xuefeng also disdained words and concepts, relying instead upon direct experience. Yunmen's time with these two teachers shaped his own approach to teaching. When he had students of his own, Yunmen was known to make frequent use of his staff and to use a shouting kind of verbal communication that pushed conventional language to its limits.

Eventually Xuefeng named Yunmen as his heir and allowed him to set out on pilgrimage to other masters and holy sites. One of the small kingdoms in the far south was established by the Liu family in Guandong Province with its capital at Shaozhou. Yunmen was welcomed to this area by the Liu family and set up in the monastery of Lingshu-yuan. Later the Liu family built a monastery specifically for him on Mount Yunmen, from which he took his popular name. There Yunmen taught for the remainder of his life, subjecting his students to the same grueling discipline to which he had been subjected. After his death, his body was lacquered and thus successfully mummified and has survived until the present day as an object of veneration.

禪

TEACHINGS *Pushing Language to Its Limits*

Yunmen never taught or gave instructions in the conventional sense. On one occasion he said to his monks: "Why are you all aimlessly coming here looking for something? I only know how to eat and shit. What use is there in explaining anything else?" In a similar vein he said, "It is better if I do not speak and thus deceive you. . . . You have to break through on your own."

Even when Yunmen did speak, much of what said was incongruous, irrational, and paradoxical. He did not use language as a way to convey conceptual meaning. Rather, he used words as a psycho-spiritual tool to push his students to the edge of conventional thinking and then beyond it. He often confronted students with illogical, apparently meaningless statements, which concealed a profound truth. For example, "a good thing is not as good as nothing." He was also famed for giving unusual if pithy answers to their questions, by which he tried to shake them out of their complacent ways of thinking. He referred to these answers as his "one-word barriers"—challenges to break through to the true experience of Enlightenment by one's own efforts.

For instance, he was asked, "What is the teaching that transcends even the Buddha and the patriarchs?"

He replied, "A sesame bun."

What more can one say?

Though Yunmen's tactics might seem strange to us, the use of paradoxical language in such scriptures as the Diamond Sutra

禪

is common in the Mahayana tradition. Its purpose is to show that the experience and "content" of Enlightenment cannot be expressed in normal discourse. The Buddha himself said that some of the questions he was asked simply cannot be answered. Many metaphysical questions, he explained, have four possible answers, all of which are wrong! For instance, if the Buddha were asked if he would exist after his physical death, he would reply that it is impossible to say that a Buddha does exist after death, does not exist after death, both does and does not exist after death, or neither exists nor does not exist after death. The Buddha's point is that such a question cannot be answered using language that expresses concepts in conventional ways. Any answer to such a question falls into the trap of dualistic, "either-or" thinking, the very thing that Zen Masters urged their students to abandon. Thus Yunmen's off-the-wall answers were designed to push his students beyond dualistic concepts into the freedom and spaciousness of enlightened perception.

As we have seen, many Zen Masters before Yunmen, such as Zhaozhou and Linji, also made strange statements and engaged in unconventional dialogues with their students and other masters. In an attempt to recapture something of the quality of these and other great masters, printed collections of the sayings and lectures of the masters active during the Tang Dynasty, which came to be regarded as the Golden Age of Zen China, began to circulate in Zen circles. As much as historical documents, these collections were widely regarded as teaching tools. The illogical nature of the dialogues was seen as a potent way of avoiding conventional ideas and rationalizations. The idea was that by intensively focusing attention on one of these sayings, it would be possible to tune into the state of mind that gave rise to the saying in the first place. Since the statements were assumed to be products of the enlightened mind of a master, by pondering the words, a student might not only break through to an understanding of the meaning of the statement, but also achieve a similar state of awakening.

To help in this process, a number of collections of the best-loved and most effective dialogues were compiled and printed, such as the famous Blue Cliff Record (*Biyan Lu*) or the Gateless Barrier (*Wumenguan*). Each contained dozens of such dialogues, with explanatory comments or verses—equally enigmatic in many cases—by their compilers. Through these compilations, the use of dialogues and sayings attributed to the Zen Masters became popular tools for meditation as well as ways of ascertaining a student's degree of insight and realization. Used in this way, any such dialogue became known as a *gong-an*, or *koan*, to use the better-known Japanese term. The word *gong-an* was derived from Chinese jurisprudence. It refers to the study of a model case by student lawyers. The use of koans ultimately became a central feature of Zen practice, especially for the Linji school in China and its Japanese continuation, the Rinzai school.

禪

LESSON *Koans and Culture*

Yunmen's dialogues are greatly valued in the koan collections. His words are included more often than those of any other master. When we try to understand Yunmen's sayings, of course, we encounter several obstacles. Yunmen's dialogues were products of a particular cultural environment accustomed to verbal challenges and cryptic allusions. When we read them out of context, or from our modern point of view, the way of thinking that produced Yunmen's words seems almost incomprehensible.

The difficulty of communicating across cultural barriers can be seen from the following story. A few years ago a famous Zen Master and a Tibetan lama met for the first time. The Zen Master, perhaps wishing to test the lama's level of realization, held up an orange and asked, "What's this?"

The lama, not accustomed to this type of discourse, turned to his companions and said, "What's the matter? Hasn't the poor fellow seen a orange before?"

Another obstacle is that by their nature, koans are intended to push us beyond rational thought. It's impossible to read a book without engaging our rational understanding or regarding words as conveyers of meaning. Thus trying to learn about koans from reading a book is like trying to learn to dance or to ride a bicycle by reading a set of instructions. To get the hang of it, you simply have to do it!

Finally, as Yunmen reminded us, "You have to break through on your own!" Thus any explanation I can provide of a koan will be my explanation, not yours. But to give you a taste of what working with a koan is like, here is one of Yunmen's famous replies:

One day a monk asked Yunmen, "What is the Buddha?"
Yunmen replied, "A dried shit-stick."

In conventional Buddhism, the Buddha is the most sacred being, deserving of absolute respect and reverence. Yet Yunmen defines the Buddha as a disgusting everyday object with which all monks would be familiar. Chinese Buddhist monasteries had no toilet paper—a Chinese innovation that had not yet been invented. Instead monks used a disposable flat stick—roughly the size and shape of a wooden chopstick—to clean themselves after using the toilet.

In considering this koan, first ask yourself how you would have replied. Remember that you are not writing a definition for a dictionary. Your answer should be of life or death importance to you. Moreover, keep in mind that anything you say will not capture the essence of the real Buddha, but be merely your

禪

limited conception of the Buddha. To know the real Buddha, you need to be enlightened yourself and move beyond dualistic categories and concepts.

So, what is the meaning of Yunmen's definition? Try thinking about this paradox yourself. Don't be satisfied with the first answer that comes to mind, but keep working about it, allowing the question to arise in your mind many times during the day as you go about your activities. Eventually, the aptness of Yunmen's reply will dawn on you, and you will begin to see things a little as Yunmen saw them.

禅

Myoan Eisai *(1141-1215)*

*Practicing a moral code leads to internal harmony
and peace of mind.*

When Buddhism reached Japan in 538 CE, it soon attracted considerable interest among educated Japanese, eager for any new learning coming across the Japan Sea from China. In the early years of Japanese Buddhism, some forms of devotional Buddhism were practiced, but overall it was scholastic Buddhism that took root in the new capital of Nara. There, a small but enthusiastic group of monks lived in several splendid temples built with imperial patronage. From among their number, a few monks with the greatest promise accompanied the Japanese ambassadors on the dangerous journey across the sea to China.

As the Japanese state grew, more monks were able to make the trip to China. Some spent decades there at the feet of the great Zen Masters, while a small number of courageous Chinese monks also traveled to Japan. Yet, for centuries Zen made very little impact in Japan. To be sure, there were some monks who tried to introduce Zen into Japan, such as Dosho (628-670), who studied with the fourth Zen patriarch Daoxin, and Saigyo (767-822), the illustrious founder of a Japanese form of the Tiantai school, known in Japan as *Tendai*. However, with the collapse of the Tang Dynasty in China, Japanese contact with the mainland all but ceased for several hundred years.

The modern history of Zen in Japan begins in 1189, when the self-taught Japanese Zen Master Dainichi Nonin (dates unknown) sent two of his students to China to get Zen teachings

of the Linji lineage from a disciple of the famous Chinese master Dahui Zonggao (1080-1163). Though Nonin and the school of Zen that he established in Japan have been all but forgotten, his success in founding several centers for Zen practice laid the foundation for later schools of Zen in Japan led by Eisai and Dogen.

Myoan Eisai, the son of a Shinto priest, entered monastic life at Mount Hiei, headquarters of the Tendai school. He was thoroughly trained in the extensive Tendai curriculum, which combined studies of the Vinaya and scriptures such as the Lotus Sutra with the esoteric doctrines and practices of Tantric Buddhism. During those years, the monastic community in Japan was characterized by political scheming and laxness in practice. Disillusioned with this state of affairs, Eisai traveled to China to seek out authentic and dynamic teachings. This visit, made in 1168, was more like a sightseeing trip to various holy places such as Wutaishan and Mount Tiantai. After six months, Eisai returned to Japan, bringing with him bundles of the latest Buddhist writings and a profound impression of the vitality and popularity of Zen throughout China. He settled on the southern Japanese island of Kyushu and, for the next twenty years, immersed himself in the study and practice of Tendai doctrines and rituals. But all the while, the memory of Zen in China haunted him.

Finally, at the age of forty-seven, he set out once again to travel westward. This time, he set his sights further afield. Since Buddhism was flourishing in China, he reasoned, how much

禪

more vital would it be in India, the very font of the Buddha's teachings. Eisai must have been a very brave and determined man, for no Japanese monk ever reached India alive. Even crossing over the Japan Sea to China was perilous, as over a third of the ships that attempted the voyage never arrived. Despite the dangers, Eisai arrived safely on the mainland. There, authorities refused to grant him the necessary permits to travel to India, and he was forced to remain in China. Ironically, had he reached India, he would have been shocked to discover that Indian Buddhism was all but destroyed, caught between the hammer of Muslim invaders and the anvil of resurgent Hinduism. While in China, Eisai engaged in Zen training under Xu'an Huaichang, a master in the Linji school, and achieved a profound awakening using the koan technique then very popular in China. After four years with Xu'an, Eisai returned to Japan, armed with a certificate confirming his enlightenment and authorizing him to teach Zen.

When he returned to Japan in 1191, Eisai began teaching the Linji way of Zen as he had learned it, gathering a small group of keen students around him. With the support of the shogun Minamoto Yoritomo, Eisai founded the first monastery dedicated solely to the teaching and practice of Zen, Shofukuji on the island of Kyushu. Later, Eisai traveled to Kamakura in 1199 where the Minamoto family had established itself as the de facto rulers of Japan after their victory in a civil war some years earlier. As hardy warriors, the Minamoto family and their supporters felt little drawn to the Buddhist schools that had found favor at court, but the austerity and discipline of Eisai's Zen school attracted their interest. His dream of establishing Zen as a movement that could reform and revitalize Japanese Buddhism was never realized, however, and vehement opposition to Zen continued after his death. Eisai passed away at the age of seventy-five, sitting cross-legged in meditation at one of his monasteries in Kamakura.

禅

TEACHINGS *Dharma and Political Power*

Eisai was a prolific writer whose output covers the range of Buddhist teachings in which he was skilled, including a few books specifically devoted to Zen. Among these, his Promotion of Zen for the Protection of the Country (*Kozen Gokoku Ron*) best reflects his view of the role Zen should play in the social order that was developing in Japan under the rule of the Minamoto shoguns at Kamakura.

Though religion is clearly separated from the secular state in most Westernized countries today, in the past it was common for the two to be closely intertwined. In the young Japanese state, the link between Dharma and political power was strong from the start. Secular authorities and Buddhist clergy shared the goal of promoting Japan's welfare and security. Inspired by the accounts of benevolent kingdoms in classical Buddhist scriptures, they hoped to make Japan similarly prosperous and harmonious. Both believed that the implementation of Buddhist moral ideals and spiritual goals could safeguard the country's security and that the power of the secular government should be used to support Buddhist monasteries in this crucial religious work.

However, this close connection implied a potential danger. If the Buddhist community became corrupt or grew lax in its moral obligations and its application to meditation, the well-being of the whole country might suffer as a result. Such seemed to be the case in Eisai's day. In the decades before and after the civil war between the warrior Minamoto clan and the Taira clan, lawlessness and moral lassitude swept the country, and many thousands perished through violence and starvation. Clearly Buddhism was failing to protect the country.

Eisai believed that moral laxity in the established Buddhist schools such as Tendai bore some responsibility for the violence and instability that pervaded Japanese culture. It was this belief that had driven Eisai to seek a more authentic form of Buddhist practice in China. When he returned from his second trip to China, Eisai wrote the Promotion of Zen for the Protection of the Country. The treatise had two main aims: first, to reform

禅

the established Japanese Buddhist schools by setting them an example of morally upright and authentic practice; and second, to convince the Minamoto military rulers that the best way for them to maintain their power was to support Zen officially and to establish an enlightened government inspired by Zen ideals.

Skillfully combining passages from Mahayana scriptures with Eisai's own comments and arguments, the treatise argues in favor of Zen by praising its ethics and morality. The work must have succeeded in its aims, as the new Minamoto rulers adopted Zen as their official ideology and did much to foster its spread throughout the country in the years following Eisai's death. Eisai's call for a return to traditional standards of morality and practice also resonated with many in the Buddhist world. Masters such as Honen (1133-1212), Shinran (1173-1262), and Nichiren (1222-1282) attempted to reform the clergy and to spread Buddhist teachings to a wider audience.

As a grace note to these political and moral teachings, Eisai is famed for having brought tea seeds back with him from China and for recommending drinking tea as an aid to meditation and physical health. The connection between Zen and tea in China was traditionally thought to date back to the time of Bodhidharma himself. Though tea had been imported as a medicinal product before Eisai's time, the uniquely Japanese approach to tea drinking, so influenced by Zen esthetics in later centuries, has its origin in Eisai's handful of seeds.

禪

LESSON *Shall Nots and Should Dos*

Most of the Zen Masters we have encountered so far devoted their energies to bringing about awakening experiences in their students. They made little mention of moral discipline and ethics, at times even urging their students to stop worrying about the technicalities of the Buddhist monastic code of discipline. But we should not assume that these masters did not hold and practice high moral standards. Remember that virtually all of the great masters trained in the Vinaya before becoming practitioners of Zen. Buddhist moral precepts must have been second nature to them and hardly worthy of comment.

Since most of us have not had the benefit of traditional monastic training, we have to think about moral questions. It is a basic Buddhist teaching that practicing good morality is an essential prerequisite to making spiritual progress. So, we might wonder, what kind of moral code would Eisai have recommended for us? Though we can't be certain, it's likely he would have had no quarrel with the ten moral precepts still observed by Zen practitioners in Japan today. These are:

* Not to take life or harm other beings
* Not to steal
* Not to indulge in sexual misconduct
* Not to lie or cheat
* Not to use intoxicants that cloud the mind
* Not to gossip about the misconduct of others
* Not to praise oneself while belittling others
* Not to be stingy with spiritual or material gifts
* Not to be aggressive
* Not to slander the Three Jewels
  (Buddha, Dharma, and Sangha)

If you wish to adopt these precepts, it's helpful if you think of them not only as "shall nots" but as "should dos." So, for instance, rather than simply refraining from killing or harming other beings, make an effort to protect and foster life and to prevent others from killing and harming. To do so, you could trap and remove unwanted insects from your home, support nonharming ecological initiatives, and promote nonviolent resolutions to international conflicts. Similarly, avoid stealing, including "borrowing" things you do not intend to return from work or from other people, and at the same time, cultivate generosity by giving material and spiritual gifts to others who are less fortunate. Avoid lying, but also speak out against injustice. Avoid gossip and other kinds of aggressive speech, but also be generous with praise and kind words about the efforts of others. If you take a moment and think about it, you'll probably come up with some personal "should dos" for each of the precepts. Practicing a moral code leads to internal harmony and peace of mind and creates the conditions for positive progress in your meditation and spiritual practice.

禪

禪

Dogen Kigen *(1200-1253)*

Once you aspire to become enlightened,
even if your life takes you in many
different directions, the conditions of your life
all become a practical part of achieving enlightenment.

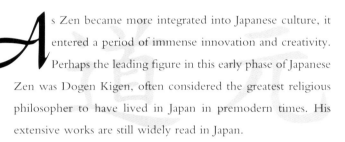

As Zen became more integrated into Japanese culture, it entered a period of immense innovation and creativity. Perhaps the leading figure in this early phase of Japanese Zen was Dogen Kigen, often considered the greatest religious philosopher to have lived in Japan in premodern times. His extensive works are still widely read in Japan.

Dogen was born in 1200 into an affluent aristocratic family. At an early age, he showed outstanding intellectual ability and was given an intensive education focused on the Chinese classics. When he was still very young, his parents died, his father when Dogen was two and his mother five years later. This harsh lesson in impermanence was long remembered by Dogen. We read in his biography that because "he understood the arising and passing away of all things, the longing for Enlightenment was kindled in his heart." Indeed his devout mother's dying wish was that he become a monk and work for the welfare of all beings.

After his parents' deaths, Dogen was taken in by an aristocratic uncle, who groomed Dogen to be his heir and successor. But Dogen had other plans. When he was twelve, he ran away and took shelter with another relative who lived as a monk near the Tendai headquarters at Mount Hiei. Dogen's persistent requests to be ordained a monk were finally heeded, and he became a novice under the personal guidance of Koen, then the head of the Tendai school.

As Dogen gained proficiency in religious studies and rituals, he became increasingly troubled by a nagging question: What is the precise relationship between Buddha-nature and Enlightenment? Someone suggested that he seek out the aged Eisai for an answer. Whether Dogen actually met Eisai is not known, but in 1217, he joined the community of monks at the Kennin Monastery in Kyoto headed by Eisai's chief disciple, Myozen. Though Myozen himself favored the Linji approach to Zen that Eisai had taught him, he also gave instruction in the Mahayana scriptures and in Tantric rituals and doctrines. These studies broadened the scope of Dogen's Buddhist education, and his later writings show signs of this considerable erudition. Appreciative though he was of Myozen's instruction, Dogen's nagging question was still not answered.

So, Dogen resolved to travel to China to seek guidance from the great Zen patriarchs. He was accompanied on this journey by Myozen himself, and the pair arrived safely in China in April, 1223. However, vigilant Chinese immigration officials kept Dogen and his party waiting on board their ship for several months before granting them permission to disembark.

During this time, a chance meeting with an aged cook from a nearby Zen monastery made a profound impact on Dogen. The monk had come to Dogen's ship to buy Japanese delicacies. Though Dogen tried to engage him in conversation, a welcome opportunity to brush up his command of spoken Chinese, the

禪

monk explained that he was unable to chat for long as he had pressing work to do in the monastery kitchen. Kitchen work, the monk continued, was his main Zen practice.

Dogen was puzzled by this explanation and asked the monk why he didn't choose to spend his last years in meditation.

In a friendly voice the monk replied, "You neither know the meaning of practice nor do you understand the words of the scriptures."

Some time later when Dogen met the Chinese monk again, he asked him what he had meant by this remark.

"The words of the scriptures are: one, two, three, four, five. Practice means that nothing in the world is hidden," said the monk.

In his later writings, Dogen tells us that as a result of this exchange, he understood that any activity can be Zen practice when it is undertaken in the right spirit.

Once he was given permission to travel in China, Dogen visited many monasteries, whose rich traditions, sincerity, and discipline impressed him deeply. Toward the end of his year-long stay, as he was making preparations to return to Japan, Dogen was introduced to the famous master, Tiantong Rujing (1163-1228), the leading figure in the Caodong form of Zen. Caodong Zen, which became known in Japan as Soto Zen, was a lineage quite distinct

禅

from the prevailing Linji form of Zen, though it, too, traced its transmission back to Huineng, founder of the Southern School of Chinese Zen. While the teaching style of the Linji school could be harsh and intimidating, Caodong is traditionally considered to be softer in its methods, though as Dogen related, Rujing was known to slap his dozing students with his slipper!

Rujing welcomed Dogen with considerable warmth and kindness. While visiting Rujing, Dogen learned that his friend and traveling companion Myozen had died. This reminder of impermanence spurred Dogen to greater effort in his practice of sitting meditation, the hallmark of the Caodong school. His hard work was rewarded by an experience of awakening during the summer retreat of 1225. Dogen was reluctant to discuss the details of his experience, but it seems to have been precipitated by hearing Rujing reprimand a sleeping monk with the words, "The body and mind are cast off in Zen. Why do you sleep?" Rujing was so impressed by the quality of Dogen's awakening that he bestowed the Caodong patriarchal seal of succession upon him with the understanding that Dogen would transmit the Caodong lineage to Japan.

Dogen remained with Rujing for several more years, deepening his experience and understanding. He returned to Japan in 1227. Unlike many monks who traveled to China, Dogen brought nothing back with him—no books, no art work, no ritual implements; only a certificate attesting to his title of succession, a portrait of Rujing, a robe that had belonged to one of Rujing's illustrious predecessors, and Myozen's ashes for interment in Japan. Dogen returned to Kennin Monastery, laid Myozen's remains to rest, and began teaching the Caodong style of Zen practice, previously unknown in Japan. The first of his many writings was composed

here, a short introduction to the practice of meditation called General Teachings for the Promotion of Seated Zen.

In 1230, meeting with hostility within Kennin Monastery and persecution by jealous monks from Mount Hiei, Dogen moved to a modest country temple, the An'yo-in, near Kyoto. Here Dogen entered the most creative, and probably happiest, phase of his life. He taught the Caodong style of seated meditation and, unusually for the time, lectured to a group of devotees that included men and women from all levels of society. It is said that he turned no one away and that everyone left brimming with enthusiasm and confidence in their potential for Enlightenment. In 1233, one of the most powerful warrior clans built a new monastery for Dogen, called the Koshoji. Here Dogen continued to teach seated meditation. Many lectures and other writings from this period have survived, forming a substantial part of his great work, known as the Treasury of the Eye of the True Dharma.

As Dogen's prestige grew, so did hostility from monks in Kyoto and Kamakura, among them many practicing the Japanese form of Linji Zen, known as Rinzai. These monks no doubt felt threatened financially and spiritually by the growing popularity of Dogen's approach. As a result, after ten thriving years at Koshoji, Dogen uprooted his community and led them in 1243 to Echizen, a desolate region on the northeast coast of Japan, far from jealous rivals. A large parcel of land had been donated there,

with sufficient funds and workers to construct a new monastery. As the monastery was being built, Dogen became depressed and noticeably bitter. Though his literary output was staggering, the overall quality of his writings fell short of his previous brilliance, and he became almost obsessive in his criticism of the Rinzai school, which he accused of neglecting seated meditation and lacking a genuine understanding of Buddhism. Fortunately, when construction of the new monastery was completed, Dogen regained his equilibrium. In 1246, the new complex, vast and virtually self-contained, was consecrated with the formal name *Eihei-ji*, "The Temple of Eternal Peace."

Dogen threw himself wholeheartedly into supervising life at the monastery, developing the rules and rituals he believed necessary for the long-term success of the new school. Never strong physically, his health began to decline, and he passed away in August, 1253. His childhood understanding of impermanence seems never to have left him, for the opening lines of a deathbed poem read:

On leaf and grass
Awaiting the morning sun,
The dew quickly evaporates away.

Eihei-ji continues to flourish as a fitting memorial to this extraordinary man, today welcoming visitors from all over the world.

禅

TEACHINGS *Treasury of the True Dharma*

The primary source for information about Dogen's teachings and philosophy is the compilation of his lectures and essays known as the Treasury of the Eye of the True Dharma. This enormous book, containing ninety-two chapters, collects writings from over a twenty-year period. A work of great genius, it was written in Japanese rather than the classical Chinese favored by Japanese intellectuals of the day. It covers a broad range of topics from instructions aimed at lay practitioners to profound if abstruse philosophical deliberations. This treasury of early Zen writings was neglected for four hundred years, until it was discovered by chance in a storeroom at Eihei-ji and published in the seventeenth century.

Though the writings in the book are various, a few key themes emerge. First, Dogen was keenly interested in the Caodong practice of seated meditation, often known by its Japanese name, *zazen*. Though the first patriarch Bodhidharma had taught the importance of meditation, the Zen lineages in China from the time of Mazu gradually came to emphasize daily activities and the use of koans instead of meditation practice, especially in monasteries affiliated with the dominant Linji school.

In his Treasury, Dogen gave detailed instructions for how to sit zazen. He first describes correct sitting posture in terms similar to the discussion in Chapter 1. Then he writes: "Now that the physical posture is in order, regulate your breathing. If a thought arises, then take note of it and then dismiss it. If you practice in this way for a long time, you will forget attachments and concentration will arise naturally. That is the art of seated meditation [*zazen*], the Dharma-gate of great rest and joy." Regular sitting meditation leads to a mental state that is a combination of relaxation and alertness, like the effortless attention we often see in cats at rest. However, we should engage in zazen without any conscious desires for future attainments. As Dogen reminded his students on many occasions, the present moment is all that is important; whatever lies in the future will happen as it should, without us hurrying it along.

Another of Dogen's frequent themes is Buddha-nature. From his writings, it seems clear that he resolved for himself the nagging question that had initially spurred his spiritual search. With characteristic brilliance, Dogen brought something new to the teaching on Buddha-nature by reinterpreting a well-known line from the Nirvana Sutra. Read conventionally, the line states that "all beings without exception have Buddha-nature." However, Dogen reinterpreted the sentence to mean, "the totality of beings *is* Buddha-nature." Thus instead of asserting that Buddha-nature lies within us, Dogen widened the scope of the doctrine to say that each being lies within a universal dimension of Buddha-nature. Dogen was perhaps the first within Buddhism to see the universe as a sacred place, its totality identical with the field of Enlightenment. Thus for him, even transitory phenomena,

禅

including those that seem mediocre or defiled, participate in the enlightened energy of Buddha-nature, which he saw not as a static condition, but as a dynamic process that manifests in the very flow of the phenomenal world. As Dogen stated, "the very impermanency of grass and trees . . . of people and things, body and mind, *is* the Buddha-nature." Practicing zazen helps us transcend our everyday ego-selves. When we forget ourselves, we become one with reality—awakened to our natural place within all-compassing Buddha-mind.

A third prevalent theme in Dogen's thinking is faith and devotion. He urged those who would follow the Buddhist path to trust in it and to believe wholeheartedly that they are held firmly *within* Buddha-mind from the beginning. For Dogen, faith is not something that can be developed through effort. Instead, it wells up spontaneously from Buddha-nature of which it is an inherent part. As one's understanding of the all-pervasive nature of Buddha-nature grows, one's whole being is pervaded by faith. Dogen also expressed deep respect for devotional practices, such as honoring the scriptures. With the notable exception of his bitterness about his Rinzai rivals, Dogen's writings are notable for their tolerance of other forms of Buddhist practice. Though the principal method he advocated was zazen, Dogen taught that devotion to and respect for the Buddhist scriptures as a source for inspiration and insight is essential. The scriptures should be treated with the greatest veneration, he wrote, since they are concrete embodiments of the Dharma.

禅

LESSON *Compassion and Insight*

What lessons can we draw from Dogen's life and teachings? Let's begin with a short biographical story that draws together a number of Dogen's concerns.

Several of the monks at Dogen's monastery had noticed a deer grazing nearby. They began to feed it scraps of food. After a while the deer became trusting and would eat out of their hands. Having taken to heart Dogen's teachings about the universality of Buddha-nature, the monks were pleased with themselves. However, Dogen was less happy when he heard about the deer. When a suitable opportunity arose, he threw sticks and stones at the deer, which ran away frightened.

The monks were scandalized by Dogen's actions and confronted him demanding an explanation. "We were kindly feeding the deer, but you have cruelly thrown stones at it so it no longer visits."

"So you think you were being compassionate, do you?" Dogen replied. "It is dangerous for a deer to become accustomed to people."

The monks protested. "We would never do anything to hurt it. We were just feeding it."

"No, you didn't intend to hurt the deer, but what if the next person your tame deer met was a hunter?"

This story highlights a common problem. We hear wonderful stories about the importance of compassion and kindness in Buddhism. Compassion almost defines Buddhism for some people. Of course, we want to develop similar love and compassion for all beings. But compassion without insight, Dogen is warning us, can do more harm than good. It is little better than a blind person fumbling in the darkness. Dogen is not telling us to restrict our compassion in any way, but he is advising us to be fully aware of its implications.

If you feel sorry for the homeless alcoholic, is it compassionate to give him money? Consider whether the money you give may help him buy the last bottle that kills him. Might it not be better to help by giving him food or clothing, gifts that cannot cause harm? At the same time, it is important that you do not become hardened or reluctant to perform acts of compassion. Beware of becoming a person who has developed great insight and knowledge but neglects everyday acts of kindness. Buddhism without compassion is meaningless; its very soul turned cold. Compassion without insight is blind and potentially harmful. Insight without compassion can lead to a callous disregard for the sufferings of others. In Dogen's view, Enlightenment or Buddha-mind is characterized by the harmonious balance of compassion and insight, which he so well exemplified in his own life.

禪

禅

Jakushitsu Genko *(1290-1367)*

Recollection of the Buddha aims to liberate one
from the cycle of the birth and death;
Zen practice seeks to realize one's primordial nature.

By the end of the thirteenth century, the political and cultural landscape of Japan had once again become unstable. The power of the shoguns, the military rulers of Japan, was crumbling, despite their having successfully repelled several Mongol attempts to invade the country. Japan was on the verge of civil war, this time between two rival imperial courts.

In this troubled time, Jakushitsu Genko was born into a branch of the aristocratic Fujiwara clan in Mimasaka, in present-day Okayama prefecture. When he was twelve, he was placed in the care of monks at the Tofuku-ji monastery in Kyoto. It is said that he became a novice more as a means of securing a good education than because of an overwhelming religious vocation. Nevertheless, a few years later, he met a visiting monk who practiced Zen meditation and experienced a conversion. Impressed by the insight and serenity of this unknown monk, Jakushitsu resolved to undergo Zen training himself. In 1305, he and a friend were accepted as trainees in Kamakura by Yakuo Tokken (1245-1320), well-known for having studied Zen in China. Jakushitsu became Tokken's personal assistant. Fifteen years later, when Tokken was dying, Jakushitsu asked his teacher for a final word. Tokken said nothing, giving Jakushitsu only a sharp slap on the face, which triggered Jakushitsu's first experience of awakening.

Tokken had encouraged Jakushitsu to travel around Japan to deepen his understanding and to learn from the Chinese Zen masters who had fled there as refugees from the devastating Mongol conquest of China. Jakushitsu, however, decided to travel within China itself, where a semblance of normality was gradually returning. Jakushitsu remained in China for six years, staying at rural temples and visiting several Zen Masters. The most influential of these was Zhongfeng Mingben (1263-1323), already well-known in Japanese circles for his efforts to revitalize the Linji form of Zen. Although we know little about Jakushitsu's experiences with Mingben, Jakushitsu expressed great respect and gratitude toward him later in life, writing that "since the time of the Buddha, there has been only one" of such presence. While in China, Jakushitsu also spent time learning to write the Chinese-style poems (*kanshi*) for which he is now best remembered.

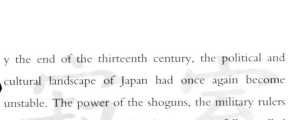

Jakushitsu returned to Japan in 1326. The manner of his return tells us much about his character. As Jakushitsu disembarked, he gave away all the souvenirs he had collected while visiting Zen teachers in China, strode away, and disappeared into obscurity. Even in China, Jakushitsu had shown a great love for rural solitude. It is most likely that he spent the next thirty-five years living as a recluse, practicing Zen and avoiding the worst upheavals of the escalating civil war. We get a hint of his feelings during this time in one of his poems: "Smoke and war is everywhere: When will it end?"

Around 1361, Jakushitsu's time of solitude ended, and he was persuaded to take up the post of abbot at a temple called the Eigen-ji, which had been built for him in the forested mountains near Kyoto. During his few remaining years, he was visited by thousands of people. Some were serious seekers like Bassui; others were basically spiritual sightseers. After five years, Jakushitsu resigned his post as abbot and retired once again into seclusion. Another poem gives us a glimpse of his feelings: "This phantom, this shadow decides to truly hide away." He died a year later.

禅

TEACHINGS *Pure Land and Zen*

Apart from his collection of Chinese-style poems and a few sayings recorded late in his life, Jakushitsu left little written record of his teachings. A central theme of these writings is Pure Land Buddhism. Pure Land has its roots in early Indian Mahayana Buddhism. As developed in China and Japan, the Pure Land school became an alternative path to Enlightenment aimed particularly at those with little time or ability to engage in more sophisticated or rigorous practices. This so-called "easy" approach became the predominant form of Buddhism among ordinary Chinese and Japanese people.

As its name suggests, Pure Land is based on the idea that certain mythical or celestial Buddhas established pure abodes under their guardianship in other parts of the universe. Through their powerful compassion for the suffering of beings, these Buddhas guarantee all people the opportunity for rebirth in one of these Pure Lands where conditions are perfect for their eventual attainment of Enlightenment. The practice required to secure rebirth in such a place is recollecting or reciting the name of one of the guardian Buddhas. The most popular of these was Amitabha, the Buddha of Infinite Light. His Pure Land, to which many Buddhists aspired, was the abode of Sukhavati.

The popular appeal of Pure Land Buddhism lay in its belief in the saving power of a Buddha. Thus it seems radically opposed to the Zen view that Enlightenment is to be achieved by one's

禅

own strenuous efforts to realize the innate Buddha-mind. During the Tang era in China, Pure Land adherents were among the most vocal critics of Zen, as can be seen in the writings of Huiri (680-748), who denounced Zen as a non-Buddhist heresy when he returned to China after seventeen years of studying Buddhism in India. It seems strange that these two rival approaches could find any common ground. But by the Song period, many Chinese Zen Masters had made their peace with Pure Land practice. This process of rapprochement continued over the centuries. Today, Buddhism in China is largely a synthesis of Pure Land and Zen. Jakushitsu encountered this Zen appreciation of Pure Land practice when he was studying in China under Mingben and other masters.

Jakushitsu saw that there was a common principle underlying both Pure Land and Zen. For him, the difference between the two approaches was basically a question of where to begin, which depended on the individual capacity of the practitioner. As he wrote:

Recollection of the Buddha aims to liberate one from the cycle of birth and death; Zen practice seeks to realize one's primordial nature. Never has it been that case that one who escapes rebirth does not also grasp their primordial nature nor that one who has grasped their primordial nature does not also escape rebirth. Therefore, even though they are different in name, Zen and Pure land practice are identical in essence.

禅

LESSON *Nembutsu*

Although Jakushitsu stressed that the real Pure Land exists within one's own mind, he also would have approved of the Pure Land practice called *nembutsu*, "recitation of the name of the Buddha Amitabha."

As in Zen, the strong motivating power of faith coupled with devotion is vital in Pure Land practice. While some later Japanese Pure Land teachers taught that reciting Buddha Amitabha's name was enough to ensure rebirth in Sukhavati, it was more commonly thought that strict observance of the Buddhist precepts of morality and the cultivation of kindness and compassion were also essential elements of the practice. In this context, Pure Land practice can be seen as a good antidote to the danger of pride. If we believe that we can rely solely on our own abilities to gain Enlightenment, we may become over-confident and arrogant, puffed up by our attainments, real or imaginary. Recalling the perfect power and perfect humility of the Buddhas can ground us in the understanding that we always need help to overcome our delusions.

The practice of nembutsu is quite simple. Sit down comfortably in meditation posture and focus for a while on your breathing. Then close your eyes and bring to mind an image of the Buddha Amitabha. He sits cross-legged, dressed like a monk, holding a bowl in the palms of his hands which are resting on his lap. He is shining golden or radiant white in color. It may be helpful to have a picture of Amitabha arranged near your practice spot to bring his image more clearly to mind. Having generated this image within your mind's eye, start reciting Amitabha's name as you breathe in and out. You can, if you wish, count your recitations on the beads of a rosary or mala. The words of the recitation are "*Namu Amida Butsu,*" which means "*Salutations to Amitabha Buddha.*" Jakushitsu would have said the words according to Japanese pronunciation as "*Naam Amida Butz.*"

However you pronounce Amitabha's name, this practice of recitation can be effective in stilling the normal busy flow of thoughts and emotions. As such, its effect is similar to reciting a mantra or meditating on the key word of a koan. You might also try reciting Amitabha's name as a way of resting after an intensive session of Zen meditation, or say it under your breath when you are out and about as a way of bringing to mind the qualities and power of the Buddhas.

禅

禪

Bassui *(1327-1387)*

Buddha-nature, the Self of all beings, is the simple Truth. From Buddhas to insects, it is the seer, hearer, and mover.

Bassui was an uncharacteristic Zen Master who preferred a wandering or hermitic life to the settled routine of a monastery. Modest and self-effacing, he attracted a following in spite of himself and inspired others by his dedication to the quest for spiritual answers.

Bassui was born in a small town located in present-day Kanagawa prefecture. His birth has a fairy tale quality. Just before Bassui was born, his mother had a frightening dream that she was about to give birth to a demon-child or changeling. When Bassui was born, she had him abandoned in a nearby field, though a family servant retrieved the baby and nursed him through infancy. Though the mother's actions sound unthinkably cruel, she was actually following a folk custom designed to trick the demons into thinking that Bassui was somebody else's child so they would leave him alone. Bassui's father died while Bassui was still very young. At his father's memorial service, the seeds of a lifelong quest were planted in Bassui's heart. The young Bassui wanted to eat the cakes laid out as offerings on the altar, but a monk told him that they were intended for his father's soul. Bassui began puzzling, What is this soul?

When Bassui was nine, we are told that he heard about the miserable kinds of rebirth that are possible, including birth as a hell being, an animal, or a ghost. Bassui became very fearful for himself and others. This fear prompted him to wonder still more: What is this soul that can be reborn into such terrible forms? As

he grew toward adulthood, Bassui began sitting for hours in meditation, still pondering the vexing question. Eventually he came to the realization that there is nothing substantial that can be called "the soul." For a while, this realization freed him from doubts.

But then Bassui chanced to read that "the mind is the host, and the body is the guest." This statement seemed to suggest that "mind" must be some kind of spiritual self or soul that plays host to a series of temporary "guests"—the bodies we inhabit during various incarnations. But what was the nature of this mind, Bassui now wondered? Bassui began to understand that what he was looking for is "what it is that sees and hears." In the hope of coming closer to an answer, in his early twenties Bassui studied under a local Zen Master, but he did not become a monk for another nine years. Even when he did take vows, Bassui was not attracted to the organized life of the monastery with its daily round of rituals and chanting. In fact, he did not even bother to wear monk's robes. All he did, day and night, rain or shine, was meditate!

One day he went to visit a hermit, Tokutei Jisha, who had lived alone in the mountains for decades just meditating. When Tokutei asked Bassui why he was not wearing robes although he had a monk's shaven head, Bassui replied, "I became a monk to understand the meaning of life and death, not to wear monk's robes." Bassui and Tokutei established a friendship that endured for years. Parting temporarily from Tokutei, Bassui renewed

禪

禪

his efforts to gain awakening and a true understanding of the Dharma. As dawn broke after one long night of intensive meditation, Bassui heard the murmuring sound of a mountain brook as it flowed over rocks, and he was suddenly overwhelmed with a deep sense of awakening.

Now thirty-one years old, Bassui traveled to Kamakura to see a well-known Zen Master, Kozan Mongo (dates unknown) for the traditional interview that would confirm his awakening. Then he set out once again to wander, visiting many Zen Masters. Because of his dislike of monasteries, Bassui wanted to live as a hermit like his friend Tokutei, but Tokutei dissuaded him,

warning him that even hermits face spiritual dangers, such as pride and self-satisfaction. So, Bassui went instead to study under the respected and erudite Koho Kakumyo (1271-1361), a member of Dogen's Soto Zen school. At first, Koho was cautious about confirming the realization of this odd man who would not even sleep within the walls of the monastery, preferring to stay in a hut nearby. But after examining Bassui, Koho's doubts were dispelled, and through his instruction, he was able to trigger still deeper levels of realization and awakening in Bassui.

After more than a year with Koho, Bassui went back to visit the hermit Tokutei. This time, Tokutei approved Bassui's desire

禪

to adopt the life of a hermit. Elated, Bassui built a simple hermitage for himself near his home town. There he lived alone for several years. This period of solitary meditation lasted until 1361, when Bassui went to pay his last respects to his teacher Koho who was dying. Though Koho counseled Bassui to join a monastery community, he declined and set out again on a journey around Japan, visiting famous masters and engaging in long retreats in various hermitages. One master that Bassui visited on this trip was the kindly Jakushitsu (see Chapter 14). Though the simplicity of Jakushitsu's style of Zen appealed greatly to Bassui and the two had much in common, Bassui did not stay with Jakushitsu, or any single master, for too long.

Bassui's spiritual travels lasted this time for seventeen years. As he traveled from monastery to monastery and hermitage to hermitage, his reputation as an outstanding teacher grew. A small group of people, both men and women, became his literal followers, doggedly trailing around after Bassui when he periodically uprooted himself. Bassui himself did nothing to encourage this attention. At times, it's said, he would even sneak away and hide from his itinerant students. But as he grew older, Bassui settled down, taking up residence in 1380 at the Kogakan Hermitage. Though Bassui may have wished to resume his solitary life, the hermitage soon became a monastery in all but name, with over a thousand monks and lay people living there in order to be close to Bassui. During this time, one of these grateful

disciples compiled the small collection of Bassui's lectures called Mud and Water.

It seems that by the end of his life, Bassui had found satisfying answers to the questions that had haunted him from his youth. Like many great masters, he used his death as a way of delivering a final teaching. After a group session of meditation, still seated, he turned to his disciples and said, "Look directly! What is this? Look in this manner, and you will not be fooled." He repeated this sentence loudly once more and then died.

禅

TEACHINGS *Doubt*

Apart from Mud and Water, the short volume of his lectures, only a few letters from Bassui's hand have survived. The central theme of his teachings, in one word, is "doubt." In Zen, doubt does not have negative connotations. Rather, it denotes a frame of mind given to intense speculation about the nature and meaning of life, Enlightenment, Buddha-nature—and everything else. Doubt develops as the niggling questions we have about life grow and grow until they become a burning need to know. But, as Bassui wrote: "Some, unfortunately, resolve their doubts after three or four days, while others take as many as three, five, ten, or even twenty years before resolving their doubts." As was the case in Bassui's life, unresolved doubts can help us overcome the obstacles, disappointments, and hardships that inevitably arise on the spiritual path and motivate us to engage in meditation, travel, study, retreats, and other spiritual activities.

Bassui's doubts about the nature of the soul matured as he grew into a more sophisticated inquiry into the nature of the mind. He used his own questions as a basis for instructing his disciples, suggesting that they repeatedly ask themselves: What is it that sees; what is it that hears? For Bassui these questions are the underlying basis of all koans. Though the precise wording may differ depending on the master, the intention of all koans is the same— to dig below the surface levels of the mind and its contents, until one rejects every limited manifestation of conceptual thought.

禅

Ultimately, as Bassui recognized, the true identity of a human being is that "suchness" from which the everyday mind arises. It is "the real Buddha, which is nothing other than the essence of all things, the master of seeing, hearing, and perceiving," though it cannot be understood or described in words.

Despite his discomfort with the routines of monastery life, Bassui accepted the need for conventional forms of Buddhist practice and understood them to be commendable ways to avoid harming others and to protect oneself from rebirth in the miserable states of existence. However, he interpreted these elements of Buddhist practice as metaphors for the philosophical aspects of Zen. For example, acknowledging that Buddhist scriptures enjoin practitioners to "receive, uphold, read, recite, expound, and copy the sutras," Bassui wrote that these activities are not ends in themselves but actually ways of "seeing into your own true nature," for "reading and reciting a sutra is to believe and understand the significance of the nature of your true mind."

At the same time, Bassui laid great emphasis upon the observance of Buddhist morality and ethics. He urged his followers to uphold the precepts, for until they achieve Enlightenment, people need the precepts to protect themselves from the karmic consequences of misdeeds. As he wrote: "Enlightenment through upholding the precepts and harmonizing the precepts through Enlightenment are different in principle, but they are just the one path after Enlightenment has been attained."

禪

LESSON *Finding a Good Teacher*

Also in Mud and Water, Bassui gave advice about finding a good teacher. He warned his followers to beware of false guides who say they teach the way to liberation, but lead instead to further enmeshment in the cycle of rebirth and its inherent suffering.

When you first set out on any spiritual quest, whether Zen or some other path, Bassui wrote, you are like a trusting infant. You are easily fooled by persuasive words, promises, and veiled threats. You simply do not have the experience or the insight necessary to identify an authentic teacher. As an initial test of a prospective teacher, "You should first clearly discern the orthodoxy of his approach." Then you should observe the teacher's disciples to see whether they have benefited from the teacher's instruction. "A truly good teacher," Bassui wrote, "does not destroy people's sight, but he points directly to their minds showing them their true nature." Moreover, Bassui counseled, you should look at a teacher's own attainments, for "a good teacher is one who combines understanding and practice and has no lingering delusions . . . he has unified body and mind, equally understands meditation and the precepts, is not moved by praise or blame."

If you are lucky enough to find a teacher who displays these attributes, you still must consider whether the teacher's personal style fits well with your own. It is your own previous karmic conditioning, Bassui wrote, that attracts you to some forms of teaching and repels you from others. As long as the style of the teacher you choose fits your temperament, many styles can bring results. Nor does it matter how many students your teacher has. Better a genuine teacher with a few disciples than a fake teacher with thousands!

Bassui warned that there are two types of false teachers: those who are arrogantly self-deluded and those who are cynically manipulative of others. The first type includes teachers who have some familiarity with the superficial aspects of the Dharma but have made a little personal spiritual progress. Such teachers may have convinced themselves that they are enlightened and superior to everybody else. Although what such self-deluded masters teach may be authentic Buddhism, their knowledge is imperfect as it is unsubstantiated by direct experience and so can mislead their followers. Though less common, the second type of false teacher includes those who knowingly pretend to be enlightened because they enjoy the power they have over the people they dupe; as Bassui says, "They pass through this world, deceiving men and women."

How might you apply Bassui's advice to your own search for a good spiritual teacher? First, carefully check the credentials of anybody who claims to be a spiritual teacher. Observe carefully for a while, asking yourself: Does the teacher's behavior match his/her words? Is the teacher affiliated with a reputable organization or movement? What was his/her training? Has the teacher been accredited by a reputable teacher? Rather than taking the

禅

teacher's word for any of these credentials, confirm them with others, if you can. Next, avoid committing yourself immediately. Take your time and watch carefully how the teacher behaves and how he/she interacts with students. Finally, and above all, use your common sense. Choosing a spiritual teacher is a bit like choosing a doctor or dentist; it's your spiritual health that is at stake!

Though Bassui does not specifically mention humor as a useful test to detect a genuine teacher, you will find that most good teachers also have a well-developed sense of humor and are not afraid of laughing at themselves on occasion.

禅

Takuan Soho *(1573-1645)*

When a person does not think, "Where shall I put it?" the mind will extend throughout the entire body and move to any place at all. The effort not to stop the mind in just one place—this is discipline.

Say "*takuan*" to someone from Japan, and they immediately think of the crunchy yellow pickled radish that is part of every traditional Japanese meal. Curiously, few of the younger generation seem to know why these pickles are so named. In fact, they were the invention of a talented and versatile Zen monk, Takuan Soho, who lived in the early seventeenth century, when Japan was gradually returning to peace under the Tokugawa regime following two hundred years of civil war.

Just who was this Takuan? He was born into a samurai family in the small town of Izushi in south-central Japan. His early childhood interest in religion led his family to place him as a student at a local Pure Land temple where he gained a grounding in basic Buddhist doctrines. Finding the Pure Land approach not to his taste, Takuan arranged to be taught at the nearby Sugyo Temple by a reputable Zen Master, who took him to Kyoto, former imperial capital and home to many prestigious Buddhist temples and schools. There in 1594 Takuan started Zen training under the well-respected master Shun'oku at the Daitoku Monastery but did not make much progress in the lax atmosphere that prevailed there.

Takuan left Daitoku Monastery to travel, studying under several masters, notably Monsai Tonin (?–1603). Tonin ran a temple school where he taught a range of studies including calligraphy, Confucianism, and poetry. Takuan excelled at these disciplines. After Tonin's death, he took up residence in the monastery,

inheriting Tonin's precious collection of books. Access to this wealth of scholarship awoke in Takuan a lifelong thirst for knowledge that he nurtured in tandem with his Zen pursuits.

Around this time, Takuan became a disciple of the austere Rinzai master Itto Shoteki (?–1606), who pushed Takuan to his limits and precipitated his first awakening experience in 1604. Following Shoteki's death, Takuan became the abbot of a small country temple, the Nanso-ji, where he lived frugally. The locals nicknamed him "the naked monk" because of an incident in which he was caught naked after having hung his single robe out to dry. On that day, Takuan had run into his room to hide from the laughing onlookers. But Takuan turned this nickname to his advantage and later said, "I'm sorry you all don't become naked. Aren't you pained by your greedy clinging to things, fame, property, and possessions? If you become a naked monk like me, you will feel better."

Takuan's erudition and dedication to Zen practice came to the ears of the emperor, who installed him as abbot of the Daitoku Monastery where he had once studied. Finding things not much changed there over the years, Takuan refused the post and went back to his peaceful rural Nanso-ji. However, the last paroxysms of the ongoing civil war erupted, and in 1615, Nanso-ji was burned to the ground. With the vigor and resourcefulness of many Zen Masters, Takuan was able to get the temple rebuilt the following year. Like other Zen monks of the period, Takuan

禅

preferred the peace and solitude of the countryside, and so he spent many of the following years traveling from one small temple to another, using the Sugyo Temple where he had studied as a youth as his home base.

The peace of Takuan's mature years was interrupted in 1627 when he became involved in a dispute between the imperial court and the Tokugawa military rulers over the appointment of abbots at several influential monasteries, including Daitoku Monastery. These appointments were traditionally the prerogative of the imperial court in Kyoto, but the military shoguns imposed strict new qualifications that made it all but impossible for new abbots to be selected. Takuan was one of those who spoke out against this interference. He was punished by being exiled to remote northern Japan. Fortunately his exile was revoked in 1632, and he returned first to Kyoto and then to his birthplace of Izushi.

When he had lived previously in Edo—present-day Tokyo—Takuan had become friends with the renowned swordsman Yagyu Munemori (1527–1607). The two carried on a lively correspondence about the implications of Zen for a warrior. Takuan's connection with Munemori prompted the current shogun, Tokugawa Iemitsu, to invite Takuan back to Edo, where he became the abbot at a temple built for him by Iemitsu on the outskirts of Edo. Takuan had taken few disciples during his life and, as his death drew near, he was not even particularly concerned with appointing a successor. He did, however, give instructions for his funeral: "Bury my body on the mountain behind the temple, throw some earth on it, and then go away!" As he lay dying, he was asked for a parting message. Without speaking, he took up his writing brush and wrote the character for "dream."

禅

TEACHINGS *Philosophical Swordsmanship*

In Takuan, we see the combination of spiritual and artistic concerns that are so characteristic of the contemporary Zen esthetic. In addition to his great learning, Takuan was also an outstanding calligrapher and artist in the *sumi-e* or "black ink paintings" so loved by Zen practitioners. His writings range from abstruse philosophical treatises to letters, poetry, and, most famously, discussions of the relationship between Zen and swordsmanship. Although he had been critical of the dedication to the tea ceremony of the monks at Daitoku Monastery, his views of this art seemed to have softened, for he was famous in his day as an accomplished and refined tea-master!

Takuan's central philosophical concern was the relationship between neo-Confucian concepts and Zen doctrines. Confucius himself lived and taught in China in the fifth century BCE, at the same time that the Buddha was teaching in India. His writings centered on right relationships and appropriate social organization. Neo or "new" Confucianism began in China in the twelfth century as a reaction to Buddhist and Daoist metaphysics. Certain key neo-Confucian concepts have marked parallels to Zen Buddhism and so would have attracted the attention of an educated thinker like Takuan. Moreover, he would have been concerned with the potential for conflict between Buddhists and neo-Confucianists, given their widespread and influential challenges to Buddhism in Japan.

Neo-Confucianist philosophy posits two interconnected cosmic principles of being: the noumenal (*li*) and the phenomenal (*qi*). The noumenal is the basic all-pervading but invisible structuring principle underlying existence. Thus it is similar to what the Buddhists call Absolute Reality, or "suchness." The phenomenal is the material manifestation of the noumenal as it takes form in the world in what Daoists call the "ten thousand things," and Buddhists term relative or everyday reality. Despite the similarity between the two philosophies, the rivalry between them in Japan generated extremely bitter written attacks. However, Takuan's aim in writing about neo-Confucianism was reconciliation and the promotion of harmony. Indeed, in other writings, Takuan also attempted to unify Buddhism with Shintoism and Daoism. Despite their apparent differences, Takuan wrote, all of these paths refer to and derive from the same underlying reality, Buddha-mind, the primordial nature of all being.

Another of Takuan's interests was the Japanese tea ceremony. The link between tea and Zen goes back to China, where the monks in Zen monasteries would hold a commemorative ceremony of tea drinking in front of a portrait of the first patriarch, Bodhidharma. These Chinese ceremonies were simple; monks would pass around a single bowl of tea which they shared. In Japan, the earliest tea ceremonies were lavish rituals enjoyed by the court nobility, but by Takuan's era, a reaction had set in against this excessive luxury. The ideal form of the ceremony

禅

was based on guidelines devised by the great tea-master Sen no Rikyu (1521-1591). As standardized by Rikyu, the ceremony took place in a small plain room adorned with nothing more than a single flower in a vase in the wall niche, or *tokonoma*, perhaps with a choice piece of calligraphy hanging behind it. Utensils such as the tea container and bowls were chosen for their conformity to the most refined ideals of simplicity and restraint. Because of the focused attention of participants and the simplicity of the tea room, the ceremony greatly resembled a Zen meditation session.

However, Takuan is best known in present-day Japan for the essays and letters he wrote at the request of the brilliant swordsman, Yagyu Munemori. Though Takuan was not in any sense

a warrior and probably never wielded a sword even in play, he was able to make useful observations about the value of Zen to confronting danger, which were of particular interest to warriors like Munemori. The connection between Zen and the martial arts dates to the early Kamakura period (1185-1333), when Eisai popularized Zen teachings among the warrior caste (see Chapter 13). Faced with the prospect of imminent death, a samurai needs to maintain the highest level of awareness if he is to survive combat. The Zen concept of no-thought was attractive as a way to develop "all-round awareness," in which attention pervades your entire body and its surroundings without being fixed on any single object so as to allow an immediate response to any situation.

Takuan eloquently described the martial application of this state of mind: "When you see with a quick glance the sword of your opponent raised to strike you, if you think about parrying the blow with your sword, your actions will be impeded, and you will die." Instead, Takuan counseled, the warrior should allow his mind to flow without attachment to thoughts and emotions: "Even when you see the sword of your opponent descending, do not fix your mind upon it and do not think about adjusting to the speed of your opponent's sword in order to return the blow—give up all distinctions and plans!" Thus, to attain victory in combat, a warrior should focus neither on himself nor on his opponent but allow the body to react without the interference of conceptual thought.

禅

LESSON *Wielding the Sword of Insight*

One of Takuan's essays on swordsmanship is called The Mysteries of Unmoving Insight. In Mahayana Buddhism, you might recall, the term *insight* refers to understanding the true nature of reality. This understanding is often symbolized by a sword. In Japanese Buddhist mythology, the sword of insight is wielded by the fearsome protector deity Acala, whose name means "unmoving." This sword can cut through the tangle of thoughts and negative emotions that so often ensnare us.

Though we are not samurai, our actions and reactions are frequently limited by hesitation, attachment, and anger. Though we do not often face a death-dealing opponent, our normal confused thinking processes can put us in danger in many everyday situations. The same mind-body discipline Takuan prescribed for warriors can help us whether we are driving a car in a rainstorm or confronting a would-be mugger. The trick, as Takuan explained, is to allow the mind to flow where it will, without conscious, and therefore potentially deluded, control:

When a person does not think, "Where shall I put it?" the mind will extend throughout the entire body and move to any place at all. The effort not to stop the mind in just one place— this is discipline. Not stopping the mind is object and essence. Put it nowhere, and it will be everywhere. Even in moving the mind outside the body, if it is sent in one direction, it will be lacking in nine others. If the mind is not restricted to just one direction, it will be in all ten.

Imagine how this mind-body discipline might help you cope with potential danger. When a life-threatening situation arises, if you allow fear or anger to surge through you, your body cannot respond properly to the situation at hand. An attitude of alertness and inner calm is a most powerful weapon of self-defense. It allows the body to do what it has been trained to do, whether that action is steering the car around obstacles or staring down an attacker with an attitude of nonthreatening self-assurance.

A famous story about the rivalry between the swordsman Yagyu Munemori and the young samurai Miyamoto Musashi (1584-1645), now renowned as the author of *A Book of Five Rings*, illustrates the thinking behind the Zen approach. One day Musashi challenged Munemori to a contest to see whose swordsmanship was superior. Musashi dipped his sword into a brook and cut a floating leaf in two as it brushed against his sword. In turn, Yagyu Munemori's dipped his sword into the brook. In his case, however, the leaf floated around his sword. Arrogantly, Musashi claimed that his use of the sword was superior. But Munemori, trained in Zen mindfulness, calmly explained that this was not the case. The Zen warrior saves lives by not using his sword, deflecting the attacks of enemies through his calm and centered spiritual presence!

禪

禅

Bankei Yotaku *(1622-1693)*

All things are resolved in the unborn.

By the early seventeenth century, the civil wars that had torn Japan apart for several centuries had ended, and the country entered a period of stability. The victorious Tokugawa family moved the capital to Edo, present-day Tokyo, and set about repressing any threats to its dictatorial rule. For Buddhism, life under military rule brought mixed blessings. On one hand, monks could follow the Dharma in peace and receive visitors from abroad. Monks traveling to Japan from Ming China stimulated a revival and a new diversity in Zen doctrines and practice. At the same time, religious activities were strictly controlled by civic authorities. The repression of the budding Christian community in Japan was typical of the deep suspicion of nonstandard views that tended to stifle unconventional expressions of spirituality. It is against this backdrop that the life and achievements of Bankei Yotaku must be viewed.

Bankei was the son of a masterless exsamurai who had become a doctor in the central province of Harima, near present-day Kobe. When Bankei was ten years old, his father died, and his elder brother took over as head of the family. Like his father, Bankei's brother was a priggish moralist, a paragon of Confucian virtues. Bankei, on the other hand, was mischievous, unruly, and defiant. He hated studying in school. Nevertheless, one day he chanced to open one of the Confucian classics, The Great Learning, and was immediately struck by its opening line: "The way of great learning illuminates illustrious virtue." What, Bankei wondered, was meant by "illustrious," or as some translators put it, "bright virtue"? Though only eleven, Bankei asked everyone he met to explain this key Confucian concept, from his teacher to neighboring Confucian "experts." But no one could explain the idea to Bankei's satisfaction. Frustrated, Bankei refused to go back to school. He even swallowed a handful of poisonous spiders in an attempt to kill himself! Thrown out of the family home by his stern brother, Bankei sought out a Zen teacher, as it had been suggested that if anybody knew the answer to his question, it would be a master of Zen.

As there were few Zen temples in the area where Bankei lived, he studied for a while at a Pure Land temple. Later, he stayed at a Shingon temple, where he was introduced to the esoteric doctrines and rituals of this Japanese form of Tantric Buddhism. Though still not satisfied with

禪

the answers he was getting, Bankei had learned enough to know that meditation training might help him. Now sixteen years old, Bankei traveled to the Zuio-ji temple, where he placed himself under the tutelage of the Zen Master Umpo Zensho (1572-1653). Convinced at last that he had found the path that would lead to the answers he sought, Bankei became a monk under Umpo's mentorship.

In 1641, Bankei set out on a grueling, four-year journey of self-discovery, sometimes traveling for days without food or shelter and sitting up many nights absorbed in deep meditation. Despite these hardships, Bankei still did not find his answer. Returning to Umpo's temple, Bankei secluded himself in a hut and pushed himself harder than ever. By 1647, exhaustion and poor diet had brought him to the brink of death. Lying on the floor of his hut, he was too weak and ill even to swallow. But then something extraordinary happened. Bankei's own words describe it well: "I felt a strange sensation in my throat. I spat against a wall, and a mass of black phlegm, as large as a soapberry, rolled down the side. Just at that instant, I realized what it was that had escaped me until now: All things are resolved in the unborn." This cathartic insight, heaved up as it were from his core, was to become the basic theme of Bankei's later teachings.

When he reported to Umpo what he had experienced, Umpo was very pleased. He recognized that Bankei had achieved a genuine awakening. What Bankei needed now was the chance to deepen his insight. In 1651, Bankei heard that a Chinese Zen master, Daozhe Chaoyuan (?–1662), had arrived at Nagasaki. Bankei made his way there to consult with him. Initially,

禅

Daozhe was cautious about certifying Bankei's awakening. But over the following months, he got to know Bankei better. When Bankei experienced a second powerful awakening experience, Daozhe wrote out a certificate attesting to his realization. True to character, Bankei snatched the certificate from Doazhe's hands and tore it up. Ever unruly and defiant, Bankei had no need of written certificates!

After about a year with Daozhe, Bankei returned to the province of Harima and began tentatively to teach. However, his unconventional ideas about what he called "the unborn" aroused suspicion among his relatively sophisticated listeners. So, Bankei moved up into the mountains to teach the peasants. When he spoke to these simple people in everyday language about the unborn mind, his teachings were better received.

The remainder of Bankei's life was spent as a teacher in one temple or another, supported by appreciative patrons. Though constantly plagued by ill-health, including coughing fits and severe stomach cramps, he attracted a devoted following, said to have numbered over fifty thousand. Wherever he spoke and to whatever audience, his teaching style was always simple and direct. He loathed the physical tactics, including beatings and loud shouts, that many Zen masters employed. All he demanded from his followers was strict morality and intense dedication to the Dharma.

By 1693, his health was failing rapidly. Such was the love and respect he kindled in his disciples that they resolved to build a commemorative pagoda for him. A large group of ordinary men and women, young and old, worked long hours on the construction of the pagoda, in the hope that the merit of their efforts would somehow prolong their beloved teacher's life. When the end came, Bankei was asked for his final words. With characteristic simplicity, he said that his everyday life would suffice as his spiritual legacy.

禅

TEACHINGS *The Unborn*

Though Bankei attracted huge crowds of devotees during his lifetime, he did not found a lineage or school of Zen. The man himself was everything, and when he died, his message was largely forgotten. In the mid-twentieth century, the great Zen popularizer Daisetsu Suzuki (1870-1966) discovered Bankei and introduced his teachings to appreciative audiences in Japan and the West. The irony of this pairing of Zen Masters would not have been lost on Bankei. While Bankei was disdainful of koans in his own practice and teaching, Suzuki was a great advocate of the Rinzai koan method.

In another way, however, Suzuki's discovery of Bankei was entirely appropriate, as Bankei himself was a great popularizer of Zen ideas. By the seventeenth century, Zen had become formalized in China and Japan and had lost much of its creativity and effectiveness. Worse still for ordinary Japanese practitioners, the classical literature of Zen was still read and quoted in Chinese language and style. Bankei deliberately rejected the copying and recitation of such writings, calling them "the dregs and slobber of old Chinese patriarchs" that were being used by inferior teachers to hide their ignorance. Instead, Bankei chose to describe Zen concepts using the everyday language of ordinary people, as masters such as Linji once had done. His aim was to reach those people who were being neglected by the formal religious teachers and institutions of the time.

The central theme of Bankei's spiritual message can be summed up by his favorite concept: "the unborn." Though he claimed that his understanding of the idea was unique, the concept itself was not new in Buddhism. In early Mahayana writings, the term *unborn* is often used to mean "the underlying emptiness or lack of intrinsic reality of all phenomena." It is the primordial state of all things as perceived by enlightened beings. The term unborn would also have been familiar to Bankei from other sources. Most notably, it was used by followers of the esoteric Shingon school to describe the mantra sound "A" (pronounced "Ah") which they taught was a manifestation of primordial or "unborn" enlightenment—the natural underlying state of all beings. As we have seen, Bankei spent time during his youth in the company of Shingon monks, who would have introduced him to the concept and to meditation on the sound.

So what did Bankei mean by "the unborn"? Though Bankei used the term as a synonym for the more familiar idea of Buddha-mind or Buddha-nature, it seems that few people understood the way he applied it. As Bankei recounts, "when I was young, nobody understood me; when they heard me, they thought I was a heretic or a Christian." But as he grew older, Bankei became more skilled in explaining his insight and won many disciples. We all use the word *unborn* without really knowing what it stands for, Bankei explained, for that which is truly unborn is inexpressible and can only be experienced. The unborn is nothing

禅

less than "the ground of everything, the beginning of everything." It is "the foundation of all the Buddhas." In other words, Bankei was telling us, it is no wonder that our ordinary minds cannot understand what is meant by "the unborn" and that ordinary words cannot capture its meaning, for it encompasses everything that exists on both the absolute and the relative levels of being.

Despite this all-encompassing definition, to Bankei there was nothing mysterious or mystical about the unborn, for everybody has it! In fact, we have had it from the first moment of life. In one of his important sermons on the subject, he said, "Buddha-mind is inherent in people from their parents. Nothing else is inherent. This Buddha-mind inherent from their parents is unborn; it enlightens the mind." Thus for Bankei, the unborn Buddha-mind is virtually our birthright. The only certainty in life, the unborn is always present, though it is often hidden under the welter of delusions and negative emotions.

Bankei has an interesting and somewhat unorthodox idea about how the Buddha-mind gets hidden. Most conventional Buddhist

禅

schools emphasize the inherited burden of karmic energy that we carry from one lifetime to the next. These karmic imprints from past deeds predispose us to various kinds of negative thoughts and actions. Like many a modern therapist, Bankei pointed the finger of blame at our parents! As he wrote, "Due to the faults of the people who raise you, somebody who was abiding in the Buddha-mind is turned into a first-class unenlightened being." For Bankei, babies come into the world with their minds in direct communion with unborn Buddha-mind. Gradually, the bad example of parents and guardians conditions and corrupts the mind so that it loses this connection. Bankei held up the example of small children as an ideal model for adults to emulate. Like Christ, he urged his followers to be like "little children of three or four who are at play."

In his dealings with students, Bankei always showed great gentleness and avoided extremes; not for him the violence of some Zen Masters. In fact, he was sometimes accused of making life too easy for his students. Once someone chided Bankei for letting his monks doze while they were meditating. His reply was very revealing: "I don't encourage people to sleep, but it is terribly wrong to hit them . . . When that monk is sleeping, do you think he is a different person? . . . When people are asleep, they're sleeping in the Buddha-mind; when they are awake, they are awake in the Buddha-mind." Here, again, we see Bankei's insistence that the unborn Buddha-mind pervades all beings at all times. If we can but develop trust that Buddha-mind is inescapably present, we will always do the right thing. As Bankei once told a visitor, "Around here, if somebody has something to do while they're sitting, they're free to get up and do it; it's up to them, whatever they have a mind to do."

Bankei's approach to Zen practice did not involve the use of koans. He believed that koans were relevant only to the original participants. A conversation between an ancient master and a student might tell you something about the master's frame of mind at the time, Bankei complained, but what can it tell you about yours now? When a puzzled student once asked Bankei why he did not use koans to instruct his pupils, he was told, "Here in my place we don't study old wastepaper." On another occasion, Bankei was even more scathing in his description of koans and quotations from the old Chinese masters. Relying upon such words would be like "feeding people poison," Bankei said with characteristic directness.

Similarly, while Bankei did not speak negatively of formal zazen meditation, he did not go out of his way to insist that his students practice it. The real meaning of zazen is not a rigid posture or concentration, Bankei explained, for "it's the Buddha-mind that sits at rest." Thus zazen, he continued, shouldn't be "limited to the time you sit meditating." Naturally, then, Bankei did not get angry if a practitioner dozed off during meditation, for it's also the Buddha-mind that is sleeping!

禅

LESSON *Everyday Life in the Unborn Mind*

If Bankei did not teach the use of koans and did not insist on meditation, how did he expect people to get in touch with Buddha-mind? Since the unborn, or Buddha-mind, is not mysterious or mystical, with the right attitude it can be accessed quite easily by ordinary people, without special spiritual techniques. The trick, it seems, is to go about your everyday activities with mindful attention and without allowing your actions to become defiled by anger and other negative emotions.

Bankei was expert at expressing this advice in terms simple people could understand and put into practice. When a farmer asked Bankei for advice about his tendency to anger, he was told:

Since all people are endowed with the unborn Buddha-mind from their birth, you are not now seeking it for the first time to follow it. If you carry out your chores with all your energy, you are cultivating the unborn mind. If while hoeing in the field, you speak with people and hoe at the same time, then you are hoeing while you are speaking and speaking while you are hoeing. But if you hoe in anger, your work becomes evil deserving of punishment in hell and your work is laborious and painful. If you hoe without the clouds of anger and other defilements, your work will be pleasant and easy. It becomes work of the unborn, unmoving Buddha-mind.

Rather than engaging in esoteric practices, Bankei was saying, your spiritual work can consist of living everyday life in the unborn mind. Since the unborn mind is pure and undefiled, eliminating negative states of mind moves you into closer connection with it. Often, Bankei explained, you have a choice about how you act or react. As he often told people, you become angry because you *choose* to be angry. One such troubled man protested, telling Bankei that though he didn't intend to get angry, other people just made him mad. Bankei pointed out the fallacy of this reasoning. You choose to be angry, he explained, because of your mistaken and self-centered belief that you need to look after "number one"—your precious ego or sense of self. Anger, greed, lust, jealousy, and other negative emotions that arise from ignorance lurk just below the surface, ready to burst forth when you allow them to do so. Bankei's solution? Use your insight to see that these negative emotional states are not really you. You are the unborn, primordial Buddha-mind. It is the precious ego you think you are protecting that is an illusion.

Since you have a choice about how to live, Bankei counsels, why not choose to live everyday in the unborn mind? If you get in the habit of paying mindful attention to whatever you are doing and avoiding negative emotional states, it won't take long for you to discover a new and extraordinary way of living. In one lecture, Bankei suggested:

禅

First stay in the unborn for thirty days; those who are accus-tomed to living for thirty days according to the unborn will thereafter live spontaneously in this way. . . . They will realize that such a life is necessary, and they will feel extraordinarily well.

. . . We would do well to try to live everyday in the unborn, and then there will be no need to strive further. For as Bankei said, "Rather than trying to *become* a Buddha, try taking the short cut and *remain* a Buddha."

禅

Hakuin Zenji *(1689-1769)*

The limitless sky of meditation.
The clear moonlight of wisdom.
The truth revealed as eternal stillness.
This earth is the pure lotus-land.
This body is the body of the Buddha.

Just as Dogen was instrumental in revitalizing the Soto form of Zen in Japan, Hakuin Zenji played a similar role with respect to Rinzai Zen. His efforts ensured the survival of this Zen lineage as a vital spiritual force to the present day.

Though a number of brilliant Zen Masters were active during the early years of the Tokugawa period (1600-1868), social changes, such as state control of religious groups, diminished the creativity and vitality of many traditional forms of organized Buddhism. When Hakuin was born in a small village in present-day Shizuoka prefecture, Rinzai Zen was in serious decline, in danger of disappearing from the spiritual landscape. Like many other notable Japanese Zen Masters, Hakuin was physically weak but intellectually gifted as a child. Like them, too, he questioned the nature of human existence from an early age and worried about his own fate in the scheme of things.

Hakuin's mother first planted in him the seeds of faith in Buddhism. When he was still a small child, Hakuin was disturbed by evidence of the ephemeral nature of existence. It is said that even shifting clouds worried him. His devout mother tried to reassure him that at least the teachings of the Buddha were unchanging, and she told him inspiring stories about the Buddha and his disciples. One day, she took Hakuin to listen to a sermon by a famous monk visiting the area. The monk's subject was the karmic results of misdeeds. His detailed descriptions of the excruciating torments suffered by those who were reborn into the hell

realms utterly terrified Hakuin. Like many small children, Hakuin had delighted in catching and killing insects and small animals. Now he realized that these cruel actions would probably cause him to be reborn in one of the hells. When his mother became aware of this anxiety, she told Hakuin that faith in the Buddha would save him.

By the age of fifteen, Hakuin had concluded that he could find peace only if he became a monk. After some initial resistance from his parents, Hakuin became a novice at a nearby temple. Here he studied the Lotus Sutra and other scriptures, but he found them less inspiring than he had expected. Worse still, he read the story of the martyrdom of the Chinese Tang period Zen Master, Yantou Zhuanhuo (828-887), who was murdered by brigands. If even a great master like Yantou could not escape a painful death, what hope was there for the likes of Hakuin? The realization that being a monk was not going to save him plunged Hakuin into despair. For a while, he lost his faith in Buddhism altogether.

At eighteen, Hakuin left the monastery to study secular poetry and painting, art forms that he practiced with talent and grace in his later years. Soon Hakuin was drawn again to Buddhist teachings. One day, the abbot of a temple where he was staying took some books out of his library to air them in the sun. Hakuin was inspired by this display of the works of the illustrious masters of the past. He was drawn to select a book to study, but he did

禅

not know which book to choose. After praying for divine guidance, he picked up a book. It was a collection of Zen stories. So entranced was Hakuin by the stories of the ancient Zen masters of China that he resolved to follow the Zen path with total dedication until he achieved Enlightenment.

As a first step, he set out on a pilgrimage of spiritual discovery that took him to many corners of Japan. While he was staying at Eigan-ji, a monastery in northwestern Japan, Hakuin had his first spiritual breakthrough, triggered by intense meditation on a koan. The experience must have been quite dramatic, judging

禅

禪

from Hakuin's description in one of his famous letters: "It was as if a sheet of ice or a jade tower had been smashed with a loud crash." As a result of this breakthrough, Hakuin's fears about impermanence and the difficulty of avoiding the torments of the hell realms evaporated like the morning dew. He knew with certainty that "there is no cycle of birth and death, there is no Enlightenment one must seek." But despite the convincing drama of Hakuin's experience, the abbot of Eigan-ji declined to authenticate Hakuin's awakening. Again, Hakuin plunged into despair. He visited several other masters, but no one would confirm his realization. This refusal was all the more galling for Hakuin since, as he recounted later, he was convinced, perhaps a bit arrogantly, that he was the only person to have had such a dramatic awakening for centuries!

Eventually, Hakuin went to stay with the notoriously strict Zen master Dokyo Etan (1642-1721), who put him through several years of merciless training. Every effort Hakuin made to show his progress was dismissed, sometimes with a laugh, other times with a sound beating. Dokyo would chide Hakuin about his limitations and call him a "poor hole-dwelling devil." It seems likely that Dokyo realized that Hakuin had too much pride in his earlier experience of awakening and needed to be taught humility. Many times, Hakuin thought of leaving, but then one day, while he was meditating on his koan, he was knocked unconscious by an angry old woman. When he came to, he found that he had resolved the koan and was in a state of ecstasy! Dokyo was delighted, but still, when Hakuin left some months later, Dokyo did not provide him with a certificate of realization. Because of this lack, some people question Hakuin's legitimacy as a Zen Master, but actions speak louder than words, especially in Zen.

Once again, Hakuin began to wander. He continued to have wave after wave of ecstatic experiences that severely affected his health. This so-called "Zen sickness," a kind of nervous disorder, coupled in Hakuin's case with vivid hallucinations and the debilitating effects of tuberculosis, quite nearly killed him. He described feeling as if his head were burning hot and buzzing with activity, while the lower part of the abdomen and legs always felt cold. He was cured of this malady by the wise hermit Hakuyu (1646-1709), who taught Hakuin the ancient Daoist technique of manipulating internal energies through visualization. Though he had occasional relapses later in life, by age thirty-two, Hakuin was healthy enough to return to his home town, where he established himself as a leading Zen Master with several temples under his care. He became famous both for his strict training of monks and for his solicitous kindness to common people. He trained a number of outstanding disciples who ensured that his style of Rinzai Zen would continue after his death and to the present day. All currently living Rinzai masters in Japan trace their transmission lineage back to Hakuin.

禅

TEACHINGS *The Great Abyss*

Hakuin's surviving writings reflect two approaches to Buddhist philosophy and practice, one for the laity and another for his monks. In his dealings with ordinary folk, Hakuin attempted with considerable success to communicate the basic message of the Dharma in everyday language. His sermons and letters are laced with humorous stories and simple but effective songs and poems.

Though he refused to countenance the Pure Land practice of reciting the Buddha's name as did some Zen Masters, he was happy to encourage his lay followers to invoke the Buddha by reciting his name and visualizing his image. He often reminded them, however, that it is better to seek the Pure Land within their own minds than to pray for rebirth in this realm. Hakuin understood that Pure Land practice is aimed at achieving a goal.

禅

Hakuin complained in his writings of the lack of vitality of Soto practitioners: "They practice silent, dead sitting as though they were incense burners in some old tomb and take this to be the true practice of the great patriarchs." While his insights did not result in any startling innovations, Hakuin did systematize the use of koans, grading them into levels appropriate for students at different stages of development. For beginners, he recommended that they meditate on a koan made famous by Zhaozhou:

A monk asks Zhaozhou, "Does a dog have Buddha-nature or not?"

Zhaozhou replies, "Mu!"

Meditating on this exchange allows students to ponder the question, "What is Buddha-nature?" until they realize that both "It has" and "It has not" are the wrong answers to the question!

Hakuin is also credited with devising some famous koans of his own. For instance, he asked his students to meditate on "the sound of one hand clapping."

For both monks and lay people, Hakuin taught that three things are essential for success in Zen practice: great faith, great doubt, and great resolve. We have encountered the idea of "great doubt" in the teachings of other Zen Masters, such as Bassui. Though some fortunate people spontaneously experience this state of uncertainty and questioning from an early age, many do not. For Hakuin, the great resolve required to engage in rigorous koan practice is the most effective way of generating the doubt and tension necessary to break through the relative everyday mind. As Hakuin said, "Great awakening lies at the bottom of great doubt." Ultimately, Hakuin taught, awakening rewards the student with joy as great as the doubt that preceded it: "It is as though a vast, empty abyss lay before you with no place to put your hands and feet. You face death, and your chest feels as though it were on fire. Then suddenly you are one with the koan, and both your body and mind are cast off . . . then there is the great joy." As for faith, Hakuin was clear that Buddhist practice requires the radical commitment that only great faith can generate: "If you want to be in harmony with your true self, you must be prepared to let go when hanging from a precipice, to die, and to return again to life." Such faith is only born of a deep understanding of the Buddha's teachings.

禅

LESSON *Restoring the Body's Balance*

Many Zen practitioners have experienced the unsettling swirl of hallucinations, hyperactivity, and distressing physical sensations that beset Hakuin in his early years. This "Zen sickness" may be caused by the ungrounding effect of too much mental activity. According to traditional Chinese medicine, the symptoms of mental and physical illness arise from an imbalance between the body's yin (feminine and recessive) energy and its yang (masculine and active) energy. Mental activity can cause an excess of yin that overwhelms the stabilizing power of yang within the body. The overstimulating quality of modern urban life, with its rapid pace, junk food diet, and unrelenting electronic media can cause a similar imbalance in us.

How might Hakuin advise us to redress this condition? The techniques taught to Hakuin by the hermit Hakuyu were based on ancient Daoist teachings aimed at restoring the body's internal balance. Hakuyu told Hakuin that a good state of health depends on keeping the upper part of the body cool and the lower part warm. With practice, the body's internal temperature can be regulated by visualization. To try this technique:

First, sit comfortably in a meditation posture. Regulate your breathing as you learned in Chapter 1, but instead of focusing your attention on your nostrils, focus on your lower abdomen. Breathing deeply and slowly, visualize that your life energy is flowing to and gathering in an area four finger widths below the navel. This spot, familiar to anyone who has practiced a Japanese or Chinese martial art, is called the *tanden*. When you experience a sensation of warmth and energy at this spot, visualize that you are guiding the warmth and energy into your genital area and down your legs to your toes. Shifting your body's energy away from the head and into your lower extremities can help you to feel grounded, calm, and revitalized.

Hakuin also taught a visualization for rebalancing the body's energy called "the butter method." It requires a degree of creative imagination but is very effective. To practice this technique, imagine a ball of pure, sweet-smelling, soft butter "the size of a duck's egg" placed on top of your head. Now imagine that this ball of butter has begun to melt. As the butter melts, you feel a sensation of cool moistness that "seems to sink deeper and go lower and lower," past the shoulders, the chest, and the belly, "until at last it reaches the bottom of your spine." Then, Hakuin says, "Everything accumulated in your chest, all the pains in your loins and bowels will flow downwards like water, until there is a distinct sensation of energy flowing all around the body, warming your legs down to the very soles of your feet."

The next time you feel heady and ungrounded by the excesses of your life, try one of these ancient therapies for restoring the body's balance.

禅

禅

Daigu Ryokan *(1758-1831)*

Unfettered like a wafting mist
I give myself up
to where the wind wants me to be.

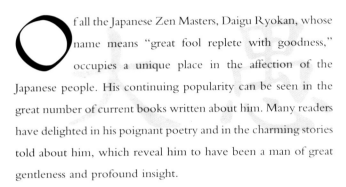

Of all the Japanese Zen Masters, Daigu Ryokan, whose name means "great fool replete with goodness," occupies a unique place in the affection of the Japanese people. His continuing popularity can be seen in the great number of current books written about him. Many readers have delighted in his poignant poetry and in the charming stories told about him, which reveal him to have been a man of great gentleness and profound insight.

Ryokan was born in 1758 at the end of the Tokugawa era. Less than forty years after his death, Japan opened its doors to Western influence after two hundred and fifty years of isolation and began its swift rise to world power. Ryokan was the eldest son of the headman or mayor of a small port, Izumozaki, on the northeastern coast of Japan, just south of present-day Niigata. Poetry, especially haiku, seems to have run in his family, which liked to trace its ancestry back to the aristocratic Tachibana clan of early medieval Japan. Ryokan's father, best known by his literary name Inan, was a haiku poet of some local renown. However, he was less able as a civic administrator. For decades, the port of Izumozaki was locked in bitter rivalry with another small port, Amaze, a few miles up the coast. When Amaze gained the upper hand in the conflict, Ryokan's father lost face, and his civic authority was considerably eroded.

Ryokan himself was a thoughtful child, attached to his mother and addicted to reading. It is said that he pored over books late into the night, burning candle after candle to the stub. While still young he attended a small academy run by a local Confucian scholar and poet, Omori Shiyo (?–1791), where he studied Chinese literature. At sixteen, he assumed his duties as heir to the leadership of his family. But around this time, Ryokan also encountered Zen practice at the Kosho-ji temple in Amaze. Monastic life must have appealed to Ryokan, for a year after starting Zen practice, he entered the temple as a novice over the objections of his parents. He wrote later that whereas most people become monks and then begin to practice Zen, he started with Zen and then became a monk. We do not know why Ryokan chose a monk's life, but biographers who knew him suggest two possible reasons: either the sight of a thief being beheaded or sadness over an unrequited love drove him to the Dharma.

While at the Kosho-ji temple, Ryokan met Zen Master Dainin Kokusen (1723-1791), who was traveling from temple to temple giving sermons. Ryokan was quite taken by Kokusen and followed him back to his home temple, the Entsu-ji, affiliated with the Soto school, in present-day Okayama prefecture. There Ryokan studied Zen doctrines and the writings of Dogen, sat in meditation, and worked hard around the temple with the other trainees. This period in his life is summed up in a poem he wrote when he was older and living in solitude:

I sat down for long meditation many a time in my youth,
Hoping to master through practice the art of quiet breathing;
Whatever virtue I have in me now to foster my heart's peace,
I owe it to the hard discipline I underwent in my youth.

Though we know nothing of how Ryokan gained his awakening, in 1790, after more than ten years with Kokusen, he was granted his certificate of realization. It included a prophetic poem Kokusen had written in Chinese:

To Ryokan, good as foolish, who walks the broadest way,
So free and easy, none can truly fathom him,
I grant this certificate with a staff of wisteria wood,
Wherever you rest against a wall, let it bring you quiet rest.

Kokusen made Ryokan head monk, which entitled him to teach at the temple. However, Ryokan decided to wander the country as a pilgrim, staying for a while on the southeastern island of Shikoku where he lived in near destitution on the seashore.

禪

In 1795, word came to him that his father had drowned himself in Kyoto after having left Izumozaki for the pleasures of drink, haiku poetry, and travel. Ryokan attended his father's funeral and then returned to the Izumozaki area as an anonymous wandering monk. By now his family's fortunes had taken a turn for the worse. His younger brother Yoshiyuki, who was head of the family, became involved in a lawsuit over the embezzlement of public funds. The case dragged on for years until, in 1810, Yoshiyuki lost. As punishment, the family property in Izumozaki was confiscated, and Yoshiyuki was banished to the ancestral village of Yoita. It is likely that Ryokan himself was not involved in this trouble, as he was living as a hermit, sheltering in various huts along the coast or in outbuildings on temple grounds.

In 1800, Ryokan moved to the area of Mount Kugami, the highest peak in a small range of mountains running parallel to the Japan Sea. The region is known for its natural beauty, with deep pine forests, mountain streams, and wild monkeys and deer. By 1804, Ryokan had built himself a small cottage on the grounds of a Shingon monastery on the mountain slopes. He wrote most of his poetry with a view of Mount Kugami. Ryokan must have loved the place, as he stayed there for the next twenty-six years. In addition to his cottage near the Shingon monastery, he had another hermitage in the grounds of a Shinto shrine on the warmer southern slopes of Mount Kugami. From 1816 onwards, this second cottage was his main home.

Life in these mountain hermitages must have been extremely tough for Ryokan. He lived on alms donated by nearby villagers and friends, supplemented by wild vegetables for which he foraged. He carried all his own firewood and water up the slopes. During the winter months, he was often snowed in for days on end. In addition to these hardships, he was plagued by a number of chronic ailments that worsened over the years—colds and lumbago in winter; and vomiting, diarrhea, and dermatitis in the hot, humid summer months.

Always modest about his abilities, Ryokan never accepted disciples. From 1815, however, a young Shingon monk, Hencho (1801-1876), insisted on staying with him as an assistant. By 1826, Ryokan's health had deteriorated so much that he was forced to leave his beloved wilderness and move to a small hut provided by his friend Kimura Motouemon (1778-1848) in Shimazaki, a few miles north of Izumozaki. Ryokan was at his lowest ebb at this time and, but for a fortuitous encounter, might have drifted downhill to an early death. However, a young widow, Teishin (1798-1872), who had become a Pure Land nun, heard of Ryokan's fame as a poet. She herself was a talented poet, specializing in the traditional thirty-one syllable *waka* style. She wanted to meet Ryokan for instruction and so, in 1827, made her way to Shimazaki. A deep friendship quickly blossomed between the sixty-nine-year-old Ryokan and Teishin, who was then twenty-nine. Teishan was an ideal companion for Ryokan, nursing him

禅

when he was ill—even washing his soiled underwear when he had one of his bouts of diarrhea—but also exchanging many poems with him.

In the autumn of 1830, Ryokan became seriously ill. Though he was unable to eat, he continued to write poetry almost to the day he died. Teishin and Hencho took turns nursing him, but Ryokan died just after the New Year in 1831, sitting in medi-tation posture as though he had fallen asleep. A few days before he died, he had written:

Not unlike the dews
Fading fast on the grass of Musashino,
All of us can stay in the world
No more than a fleeting dream.

禅

TEACHINGS *The Life of a Zen Master*

Ryokan never taught his understanding of Zen in a conventional sense, but he was an embodiment of all that is best in a Zen Master: simplicity, kindness, and a profound love of solitude and the beauties of nature. It is clear that he made a profound impact on all those with whom he came into contact, for within a few years of his death, several people who had known him were writing biographies and gathering collections of his poetry. From these eyewitness stories, we can built up a vivid picture of Ryokan. His contemporaries agree that he was the most kind and gentle man they had met. He spoke little and was not given to outbursts of joy or grief. He was happiest when he was playing ball with the children he met on his begging rounds. He usually carried several balls in his sleeves for this purpose and often played until the sun had set, forgetting to collect any food for himself. A poem describes these simple joys:

Lying alone and ill in my hut,
All day long I don't see anybody;
My bowl is left in its bag on the wall,
My staff just gathering dust.
My dreams go rambling through mountains and fields,
My heart goes back to the village to play,
And there I find all the children in the road,
Just as always, waiting for me.

On these begging rounds, he also formed strong bonds of friendship with many villagers, who were themselves desperately poor and had little to eat. These common folk shared what little they had with Ryokan. Far from being exploitive of the poor, begging one's food can be seen as a profound spiritual practice. Ryokan believed that it was a monk's duty to beg for alms, to practice such virtues as patience and humility and to give the

禅

him wherever he went, but of course, Ryokan forgot the list, as well! Though not a boisterous person, he had a childlike love of harmless practical jokes. Two stories illustrate these aspects of Ryokan's charming behavior. He had heard people say that it was fun to find money. To test this, he threw some of his coins on the ground and then picked them up. But this did not give him any pleasure. "They're just trying to trick me," he thought. But after repeating this experiment several times, Ryokan forgot where he had thrown his coins. After a lengthy search, he found them again and felt happy. "So, they weren't really deceiving me!" he exclaimed. On another occasion, Ryokan was sitting in a row with other people at a formal tea ceremony. He picked his nose and wiped a bit of snot on his sleeve. Seeing his neighbor recoil in disgust, he picked up the piece of snot and put it on his other sleeve. The man that side shrank away as well. Unperturbed, Ryokan picked up the bit of snot and put it back in his nose!

Ryokan also displayed great humanity and compassion for others, as he wrote in his private jottings: "When you encounter those who are wicked, unrighteous, foolish, stupid, deformed, vicious, chronically ill, lonely, unfortunate, or handicapped, you should think, 'How can I help them?' Even if you cannot do anything, at least you must not indulge in feelings of arrogance, superiority, derision, scorn, or abhorrence, but you should immediately show sympathy and compassion. If you fail to do so, you should feel deeply ashamed of yourself."

villagers the opportunity to practice generosity and thus generate merit for future lives. For Ryokan, it was far more exploitative for a monk to live a comfortable life in a temple with plenty to eat and little contact with common people.

So unworldly was Ryokan that he was known to be forgetful. He often left something behind at a friend's house when he was visiting. A friend suggested that he carry a checklist of items with

禪

LESSON *Zen and Haiku*

Ryokan wrote hundreds of poems. Some have not survived, for he often had no fresh paper and so would write on the same piece repeatedly or else write on the walls and doors of his huts. His poems were written in an exquisite flowing calligraphy so appreciated that even during his lifetime, forgeries were in circulation. At times he wrote poems as small gifts or else was importuned by admirers to inscribe a poem on a fan. Despite this renown, Ryokan was modest about his own work; one famous verse reads:

> Who says my poems are poems?
> My poems aren't poems at all.
> When you understand
> That my poems really are not poems,
> Then we can talk about them.

But, of course, that was Ryokan speaking. Others disagreed and avidly collected all of Ryokan's poems that they could lay their hands on.

Ryokan wrote two main genres of poetry: Chinese poems called *kanshi*, and two styles of Japanese poetry, the traditional thirty-one-syllable *tanka* and the seventeen-syllable *haiku*. His usual subject matter was aspects of his solitary life in the mountains, and though most of his poems are not specifically about Buddhism, all are tinged with an undertone of deep spirituality. Of all of these styles, the brief telegram-like haiku is, perhaps, closest to the Zen manner of expression. As a final practice for this Zen Master Class, you might wish to try your hand at writing a haiku yourself.

People have been writing haiku in English since the 1950s. It is generally agreed that an English haiku should be no more than seventeen syllables in length, arranged in three lines of 5, 7, and 5 syllables. Since such precision is difficult to achieve in English, don't be too worried if your syllable count goes over a little. It is more important to get the spirit of the poem right. To get a feel for haiku, you might wish to read one of the many anthologies of haiku available in English; those by R. H. Blyth are the most exhaustive. You can write about anything, reflecting a snapshot insight or impression that strikes you particularly forcefully, though traditional themes tend to concentrate on nature. If possible, you should include a word or two that indicates the season, as in the following example:

> Temple bells die out,
> The fragrant blossoms remain—
> A perfect evening!

禪

Here the "fragrant blossoms" tell us that it is late spring. Also note the mixing of sense impressions that is so typical of haiku. The poet hears the mellow sound of the temple bell and smells the flowers. This skilful blending is considered a mark of a good haiku. Another feature of a good haiku is "cutting," the style of dividing the poem into two distinct parts that the reader must bridge with the imagination. This break can be placed after the first or second line and is usually marked in English by a semi-colon or a dash as in the haiku above. Here is another example:

The winter seagull—
No home in life,
No grave in death.

A freezing night,
oars striking the surf;
the sound of tears.

These instructions are nothing more than suggestions. The most important quality of haiku is freshness, taking a vivid but simple, initial impression and expressing it without over-working it or prettifying it in a way that destroys the Zen ideal of spontaneity. Let us take our leave of Ryokan and the other Zen Masters with a poem that expresses perfectly the Zen sensibility:

Where did my life come from?
Where will it go?
By the window of my ramshackle hut
I search my heart in deep silence.
Though I search and search,
I still can't find where it all began
And how will I ever find its ending?
Even the present instant can't be pinpointed;
Everything changes, everything is empty:
This I only exists for a moment in that emptiness.
How can you say anything is or is not?
It's best just to hold to these little thoughts
Let things simply run their course
and so be natural and at your ease.

禅

Further Reading

Great Fool – Zen Master Ryokan
Trans. Ryuichi Abe & Peter Haskel
UNIVERSITY OF HAWAI'I PRESS 1996

Basho's Haiku and Zen
Robert Aitken
WEATHERHILL 1978

Zen Teachings of Huang-po
Trans. John Blofeld
ALLEN & UNWIN 1954

*A Quiet Room – The Poetry of the
Zen Master Jakushitsu*
Trans. Arthur Braverman
TUTTLE PUBLISHING 2000

Mud and Water (Bassui)
Trans. Arthur Braverman
NORTH POINT PRESS 1989

The Bodhidharma Anthology
Jeffrey Broughton
UNIVERSITY OF
CALIFORNIA PRESS 1999

The Korean Approach to Zen
Robert Buswell
UNIVERSITY OF HAWAI'I PRESS 1983

Zen Buddhism – A History (2 vols)
Heinrich Dumoulin
SIMON & SCHUSTER MACMILLAN 1988

The Rhetoric of Immediacy
Bernard Faure
PRINCETON UNIVERSITY PRESS 1991

Zen's Chinese Heritage
Andy Ferguson
WISDOM PUBLICATIONS 2000

Recorded Sayings of the Zen Master Joshu
(Zhaozhou)
James Green
SHAMBALA PUBLICATIONS 1998

The Awakening of Faith
Trans. Yoshito Hakeda
COLUMBIA UNIVERSITY PRESS 1967

Bankei Zen
Trans. Peter Haskel
GROVE WEIDENFELD 1984

The Koan
Ed. Steven Heine & Dale Wright
OXFORD UNIVERSITY PRESS 2000

*The Northern School and the
Formation of Early Ch'an*
John McRae
UNIVERSITY OF HAWAI'I PRESS 1986

Master Dogen's Shobogenzo (4 vols)
Trans. Gudo Nishijima & Chodo Cross
WINDBELL PUBLICATIONS 1994

Three Zen Classics (inc. Linji, Yunmen, Blue Cliff
Record)
NUMATA CENTRE FOR BUDDHIST
TRANSLATIONS 1999

Recorded Sayings of the Zen Master Lin-chi
Trans. Ruth Sasaki
INSTITUTE FOR ZEN STUDIES 1975

Two Zen Classics – Mumonkan and Hekiganroku
Katsuki Sekida
WEATHERHILL 1977

Zen Teachings of Master Lin Chi
Trans. Burton Watson
COLUMBIA UNIVERSITY PRESS 1999

The Unfettered Mind – Writings of Takuan Soho
Trans. William Scott Wilson
KODANSHA INTERNATIONAL 1987

Huineng's Platform Sutra
Philip Yampolsky
COLUMBIA UNIVERSITY PRESS 1967

Zen Master Hakuin – Selected Writings
Trans. Philip Yampolsky
COLUMBIA UNIVERSITY PRESS 1971

Picture Credits

禅

Index

Note: Zen Masters with two-part names have been entered under their commonly used name, and for those Masters whose lives and teachings are presented in detail in the text, these names are shown in bold. CM = Chinese Master; IM = Indian Master; JM = Japanese Master

禅

禅